THE
SHADOW
CATCHER

THE SHADOW CATCHER

A U.S. Agent Infiltrates Mexico's Deadly Crime Cartels

Hipolito Acosta
with Lisa Pulitzer

ATRIA BOOKS

New York   London   Toronto   Sydney   New Delhi

ATRIA BOOKS

A Division of Simon & Schuster, Inc.
1230 Avenue of the Americas
New York, NY 10020

First Atria Books hardcover edition April 2012

ATRIA B O O K S and colophon are trademarks of Simon & Schuster, Inc.

For information about special discounts for bulk purchases, please contact Simon & Schuster Special Sales at 1-866-506-1949 or business@simonandschuster.com.

The Simon & Schuster Speakers Bureau can bring authors to your live event. For more information or to book an event contact the Simon & Schuster Speakers Bureau at 1-866-248-3049 or visit our website at www.simonspeakers.com.

Designed by Kyoko Watanabe

Manufactured in the United States of America

10 9 8 7 6 5 4 3 2 1

Library of Congress Cataloging-in-Publication Data

Acosta, Hipolito.
  The shadow catcher / by Hipolito Acosta, with Lisa Pulitzer.
    p. cm.
1. Human smuggling—Mexican-American Border Region. 2. Mexicans—Crimes against—Mexican-American Border Region. 3. Illegal immigrants —Crimes against— Mexican-American Border Region. 4. Border crossing—Mexican-American Border Region. 5. Emigration and immigration law—United States. I. Pulitzer, Lisa. II. Title.
  KF4848.M48A72 2012
  363.28'5092—dc23
                                        2011040948

ISBN 978-1-4516-3287-3
ISBN 978-1-4516-3289-7 (ebook)

To my beautiful wife, Terrie,
for her unwavering support, patience, and sacrifice

Contents

Contents

Introduction

THE TELEPHONE CONVERSATION on May 14, 2003, upset me. As head of the recently reorganized United States Immigration and Naturalization Service district office in Houston, Texas, I was accustomed to receiving calls with updates on developing situations at any hour of the day, but this one was different. Nineteen people had suffocated in the back of a tractor-trailer near Victoria, Texas. Among the dead was a five-year-old boy.

The eighteen-wheeler had been carrying a cargo of illegal Mexican and Central American immigrants being smuggled into the United States. When the driver realized some of his passengers had died, he panicked, uncoupled the rig, and abandoned the trailer at a truck stop. Remarkably, fifty-one people were found alive when the vehicle was discovered about one hundred miles south of Houston. Claw marks in the truck's insulation confirmed the desperation of the trapped human cargo.

As the major media outlets began contacting me for my comments on the tragedy, I recalled the times I had infiltrated smuggling rings and placed myself in the same kind of life-and-death situation.

I'm the son of Mexican-American migrant farm workers and grew up in Redford, Texas, a tiny dot of a village facing Mexico across the Rio Grande. My family alone, with my fourteen brothers and sisters, made up seventeen of the 132 residents of my hometown. When I became a special agent of what was then the U.S. Immigration and Naturalization Service, my Hispanic heritage came in handy, allowing me to look and act the part of many of the players in the high-stakes game of human smuggling: an impoverished Mexican; a callous drug dealer; an amoral human trafficker; a womanizing smuggler with a private plane; an aspiring counterfeiter. I found it hard not to empathize with the *pollos,* or chickens— the men and women who sought freedom, sanctuary, and a better life for their families in the United States—and so I spent my career chasing the coyotes, the smugglers who were often responsible for injuring and murdering the people who paid them for transport across the U.S. border. On the job, I witnessed, prevented, and avenged brutality against migrants, not only by coyotes, but also by unscrupulous members of U.S. law enforcement.

The reporters calling me that tragic May morning were simply doing their jobs, and I respected them for that. I could never convey to them—at least not on the record, since I no longer headed the investigative branch—my single-minded desire to track down the unprincipled criminals responsible and lock them up for as long as the law allowed. This was not the first mass murder of helpless immigrants that had been brought to my attention and it would not be the last.

Every time I hear about a casualty, I regret I hadn't been able to prevent it, wishing I could have been in the right place at the right time. I know that I have saved many lives and put many unscrupulous thugs behind bars, but I also realize that I am only human. I'm Hipolito Acosta and these are some of my stories . . .

Author's Note

THE NAMES OF a few individuals referenced in this book have been changed to protect their identities and personal safety.

THE SHADOW CATCHER

CHAPTER ONE

Playing *Pollo* from Ciudad Juarez to Chicago

THE CHILL OF the river cut through my body like a jolt of electricity. The night was black and starless, and the water was creeping up to my neck. I felt like I was suffocating, the coldness of the water and air were sucking the breath out of me.

My fear turned to panic as the current threatened to pull me under the surface. I was too far advanced into the river to turn back, and I was not close enough to the other bank to feel confident. Our slimy smuggling guide was moving effortlessly through the swift waters of the Rio Grande, but he did not bother to offer us encouragement. He had made this crossing many times. This was his livelihood. Behind us, closer to

Ciudad Juarez, I spotted what seemed to be a separate group of mostly women and children. The younger ones were being carried on the shoulders of their elders.

Everyone who made it this far was exhausted from days of traveling from Central America and other parts of Mexico to reach the Rio Grande. They were risking the lives of everyone in their families in the unforgiving currents. As many as four or five hundred people drown each year trying to cross the Rio Grande where it forms the border between Mexico and the United States, but many of the deaths are not officially reported or recorded.

I was thinking of my young wife and sons in Chicago waiting for me to come home from this assignment, just as the immigrants behind me must have been thinking about family they had left behind. In our own ways, we all wanted the same thing. It was just that I was born and raised on the side of the river these people were willing to risk everything to reach.

I had traveled to Ciudad Juarez five days earlier as an undercover U.S. government agent. My assignment was to infiltrate a human smuggling ring, the first time a mission like this was ever attempted by our agency. I had been forced to acknowledge that our effort in Chicago to capture and deport illegal immigrants was getting us absolutely nowhere, and I was determined to do something more proactive by going after the human smugglers at the starting points of their pipelines.

One such staging area was La Rueda Bar, a crowded, smoke-filled, downtown Juarez lounge along a drag jam-packed with similar establishments, for block after block. It hadn't taken me long to find it. It was one of the primary contact points for smugglers and *pollos* in Juarez, according to my preliminary research. I was able to pick it out from the other drinking holes along the strip by its ugly, garish lime-green color and its trademark oversized wagon wheel hanging over the side entrance. The Mexican and American patrons loitering in the shade on the sidewalk outside were guzzling cold beers or tequila. Most were completely oblivious to the human transport wheeling-and-dealing in their midst.

The city of Juarez, Mexico, is impoverished, dirty, and dangerous. It was settled in 1659 by Spanish explorers, but its population exploded in the 1970s, when streams of Mexico's migrants began arriving from all parts of the country with the hopes of finding employment at American-owned assembly plants, known as maquiladoras. These plants hired Mexican laborers to manufacture goods with American raw materials, trying to create a win-win situation for the unskilled Mexican laborers without necessitating border crossings. Despite the thousands of secure but low-paying jobs offered at the local plants, the vastly more lucrative trades of drugs, prostitution, and human smuggling attracted a ruthless criminal element to the town. Juarez was a hard-edged frontier town that was slowly drifting toward lawlessness.

The town's nightlife was not suffering though. Americans crossed one of the three border controlled bridges from El Paso into Juarez for an evening of inexpensive fun on the "Juarez Strip" that contained more than fifty bars and nightclubs offering cheap drinks, dancing, dinner, and sex. La Rueda Bar was always a particularly popular destination.

I had crossed into Juarez on two consecutive nights to stake out the location. Both times, the dive was buzzing, overflowing with locals, prostitutes in short skirts and their johns, and drunks at all levels of intoxication. I was disguised as a *pollo*, or chicken. A *pollo* is a person seeking passage into the United States illegally. They were called *pollos* because of the way they followed their smuggler like frightened chickens with their heads about to be removed. Many in the United States call them "wetbacks," a derogatory term referencing their swim across the Rio Grande. Being Hispanic, my disguise wasn't much of a stretch.

In my pre-mission investigation, I had gathered enough information from street-level informants back in Chicago, where I was based, to learn that La Rueda was a major clearinghouse for immigrant smuggling. As a *pollo*, I was the lowest creature on the human trafficking food chain. Other agents had posed as *pollos* before, but only in U.S. operations, and with backup. No agent had ever infiltrated a smuggling organization in Mexico, never mind alone.

Going deep undercover would give me an inside view of the workings of a human trafficking organization, making it easier to identify ring leaders and dismantle the organization once I had gathered enough evidence. I would be dealing with the main smugglers firsthand. I would also have to endure the harrowing journey that thousands of illegal migrants were taking daily, risking their lives to escape the misery and poverty in their homeland.

I had been working in the Chicago district office for the past several years, mainly deporting illegal immigrnts, which was frustrating. Deportation was nothing but an inconvenience, not a deterrent to desperate people. I knew that immigrants deported one day were back on U.S. streets by the next week at the latest. The smuggling that got them here in the first place was the problem that troubled me most.

The antismuggling unit had been a department in name only when my colleague Gary Renick arrived in Chicago two years before me. No agents were assigned exclusively to the unit, but there was one priority target, the Medina family. The Medinas were an extremely tight, impenetrable human smuggling and drug syndicate, well-known to INS agents in Chicago and El Paso. Their lucrative smuggling ring ran between Juarez and Chicago, and I decided to do whatever it took to take them down, including going undercover in Mexico to infiltrate their operation at its source.

The mission may have bordered on reckless, but we had no model to follow. We were becoming overwhelmingly frustrated at the usual immigration procedures, which were stale and ineffectual, almost like Band-Aids on a hemorrhage. We hungered to try something different. Since our intelligence was that the Medinas used La Rueda Bar for their base of smuggling and narcotics operations, this was the logical place for me to get at the family.

I flew into El Paso several days before the operation was scheduled to commence. My sister Minnie and her family lived there, so I stayed with them until I did some reconnaissance of the Juarez area.

On any night, La Rueda was hopping. During my two days of surveillance, I had seen peasants gathered on the street, most likely determining who would go inside to negotiate. Eventually, one of them would enter the bar, emerging shortly with a contact. They would exchange money on the street, not concerned about being arrested. Uniformed Mexican law-enforcement officials also entered and left the bar but only spent their time laughing and joking. They were likely crooked, too, probably on the take.

Brutes driving huge pickup trucks came and went throughout the night. I watched them climb out of their vehicles with.45-caliber handguns stuck in their belts. They were obviously major players for the dope dealing business that also operated from the bar.

My clothes—an old pair of jeans and a faded flannel shirt—looked like any other hardworking Mexican's, but my hairstyle was a problem. Before this case I had taken down several vengeful criminal groups in Chicago and had grown an Afro for the role. That hair blended in fine on the streets of Chicago, but here, I wasn't sure. Luckily, in the crowd of misfits, no one gave me a second glance.

I asked my sister Minnie and her husband, Dick Hartnett, to drop me off a few blocks from La Rueda. Minnie had always been a pillar of strength for our family, and being with her as I was about to enter this shadowy world was comforting. While this assignment was dangerous, having Minnie and Dick bring me to Juarez was not. Day trips from El Paso and other southern U.S. border cities were common, since shopping and meals were a bargain in Mexico. Besides, I found comfort in knowing that a member of my family would know where to begin looking for me if I encountered trouble.

No one spoke as we crossed the International Bridge into Juarez. As we neared my destination, my sister's worry-filled voice broke the silence. "Do you really need to do this?" she pleaded. "What if something happens to you? Who is going to be there for you?"

Before I could even answer, my brother-in-law jumped in to defend my decision. "He knows what he is doing," Dick said reassuringly "Somebody has to do it. He will be fine!"

"Don't worry." I smiled, placing my hand on my sister's shoulder. Reaching beneath my seat, I pulled out the small bag of old clothing I had packed for my adventure. Carrying it would make me look more like someone who had been traveling through Mexico. My sister sat there silently as I climbed out of the van. I stood on the curb and watched as she quickly pulled away. It was showtime.

I crossed the street and entered La Rueda's side door. Aside from my hair, my Tex-Mex Spanish was not the same as a native Mexican's Spanish, so I had to be careful about what I said. These people wouldn't hesitate to kill me, even if they identified me as an American undercover agent.

I advanced nervously through the crowd toward the horseshoe-shaped bar. I would have felt more at ease with a partner, but our Chicago management team decided that I would go alone because of budgetary constraints. My eyes were slow to adjust to the dim lighting. The only bar patrons who stood out through the haze of cigarette smoke were the call girls. One of my favorite songs, Ramón Ayala's "Tragos de Amargo Licor," was playing on the jukebox, but the loud laughter drowned out the lyrics, and nobody paid it any attention. I squeezed between two badasses doing shots of tequila with a couple of señoritas and sat down on an empty bar stool. I set my small *mochila,* or "tricky" bag, of old clothes, at my feet. I had brought a small .25-caliber derringer with me, which was hidden in my back right pocket.

Without saying a word, one of the bartenders walked up and stood across the bar from me. I asked him for a beer, placing a twenty-dollar bill on the bar.

"My name is Jose Franco. I am looking for someone to take me to Chicago," I said. I chose Jose Franco for my alias because it was easy for me to remember. Jose was a common Mexican name and Franco was my father's middle name.

The bartender placed a beer on the bar and took my twenty. When he returned with my change, he demanded to know who had sent me.

"Somebody at the bus station sent me here after I asked how to get north," I said, slipping him a ten from the change.

"Wait," he told me. "Let's see what I can do. When someone who can help you comes in, I will let you know."

As I looked at the faces in the bar, I felt healthy amounts of fear and respect for what I had gotten myself into. Maybe my nerves showed and helped convince the smugglers I really was just another *pollo*. They were used to seeing trepidation in the faces of the disenfranchised peasants who placed their lives in their unscrupulous hands.

I had to proceed cautiously. I was hoping to be selected by a member of the Medina clan. But whichever coyote ended up with me was out of my control, like so many aspects of this mission. I was carrying only slightly more money than I needed and I had no badge or backup to rely on if I met with trouble. I sipped my beer and casually observed the crowd. I watched five or six other *pollos* enter and leave the bar after speaking with a small group of men, presumably coyotes.

After two hours, I thought that I had either been forgotten or fooled by the bartender. I wanted to approach a group of coyotes myself, but I decided patience was a better option. Finally, at close to one o'clock in the morning, I noticed three men engaged in hushed conversation with my bartender. The bartender pointed at several people sitting around the room, and then he pointed at me. Each coyote selected one of the *pollos* and moved toward his choice. The man who came toward me had been at the center of their small group when they entered the bar. He was shorter and slimmer than the other two, but undoubtedly in charge of the posse. I recognized him. He was Jose Medina, one of the Medina family's top soldiers. I was in.

"I hear you want to go north," he said with an arrogant sneer.

We agreed on a price and I told him I would pay the whole thing when we got there.

Jose had a sarcastic grin on his chiseled face. "No, my friend, you have to pay half of the money up front, and you have to do it now. That is, if you want to go."

I hesitated, acting like I was considering my options.

"Look, you got to have faith in us," Medina coaxed. He explained the system. *Pollos* were sent off according to a combination of factors—destination, number in the group, and first-come, first-served. I would not be departing immediately under any circumstances, but I still needed to accompany him to a staging area if I was interested. At the earliest, I would be crossing in one or two days.

"You have my word," he promised. "Anyway, you can always find me here."

The ringleaders of the Medina clan made *pollos* give them a down payment and commitment fast, or else someone else moved ahead of them. I pushed my crisp dollars toward Jose Medina and ordered another beer. Two companions joined him, generously passing several twenty-dollar bills to the bartender for his cut of the referrals.

I downed my beer and got up as Jose motioned to me and a few of his other "customers." He led us outside to an idling van. I'd heard too many stories about immigrants who paid their smuggling fees and then were herded into vehicles and taken several miles outside the city to be beaten, robbed, abandoned, or killed by the side of the road. Others were never seen again. But I got into the van with the other *pollos* anyway.

To my relief, we did not leave town, but went straight to El Correo Hotel, a seedy establishment ten minutes away from La Rueda at this late hour, when the streets were mostly deserted. The dimly lit entrance hall was jammed with twenty men, women, and children ready to depart on the next trip, as soon as a guide and vehicles arrived. We walked past a small reception desk, manned by an old man snoring, his head slumped on the counter. If he was a hotel employee, he wasn't registering guests.

The word *hotel* was a misnomer. El Correo was no vacation-guide spot. It was a human-smuggling and trafficking distribution hub, used by several different smuggling operators in Juarez. Like other clearinghouses, the activities that went on there were well-known and accepted by law enforcement agents who took a cut of the profitable business. Sometimes they raided the hotels to collect payoffs from the migrants, but they were usually bribed, so they stayed away.

Jose pushed open an unlocked door that led into one of the hotel's dismal rooms. Inside, fifteen or twenty people were sleeping on the floor, either sitting in metal folding chairs or propped up against a wall, using their tricky bags as pillows. Five more people huddled on a single twin bed in the middle of the room. No one gave our group of two a second glance as we made our way inside, led by Jose. We squeezed in as best we could, stepping over people. Women clutched their children closer at the sight of Jose.

I made my way to a corner next to a young man who was sleeping sitting up. When I placed my hand down on the carpet to sit next to him, I discovered cockroaches, fleas, and bedbugs on their own bloodsucking parasitic missions. Fortunately, only a half hour after I sat down, a smuggler opened the door and summoned four *pollos* by name. One of the men got up and I claimed his chair. But by the time I departed two days later, I was still itching from head to toe.

Napping for long stretches was impossible, between the discomfort and the noise. Every two or three hours, a smuggler slammed open the door and called the names of a handful of *pollos,* who nervously gathered their meager possessions and followed him out the door in less than two minutes. By the second night, I was adapted to getting as much sleep as I could before falling off my chair.

By day three, I was one of the veterans in the room. I took a cold shower, the only kind at El Correo. Despite the November chill, the water felt good. I quickly lathered and rinsed, dried myself off, and got back into my dirty clothes feeling like a new man. I had never been in captivity before and had been amazed at how quickly freedom melted away into darkness and despair. A quick cold shower was enough to remind me how grateful I was for liberties, no matter how small.

For three days, I had been looking at the faces behind the stories of the people in the room. The sacrifices they had made to reach the United States were frightful and astonishing. Some had already lived there but had been deported after being picked up by our immigration authorities. Others were embarking for the first time. Each person had his own American dream—an education for his children, food for his family, and maybe a visit back to Mexico to see relatives, if the opportunity arose. One young man announced he would join the U.S. Army to prove he would sacrifice his life for a chance to be a citizen of the United States.

Some people in the room talked about what crossing the river was like, but I was surprised there wasn't a lot more fear. Nobody was turning back. Fear was saved for family members back in the villages with no beans or tomatoes in the garden, on the brink of starvation, and with a bleak future ahead with only the continuous cycle of sending relatives to *el norte* giving them hope. The fast currents of the Rio Grande and the untrustworthy guides seemed relatively tame.

Many of the immigrants had borrowed money at grossly inflated interest rates just to be able to afford the down payment for the trip. The relatives who were waiting for them were going to pay the rest of the fee when they arrived. Children as young as my own two preschool-age boys huddled with their mothers, oblivious to dangers ahead of them. I prayed we would all be reunited with our families, regardless of the outcome of the smuggling case I was investigating.

After I had spent three long days and nights in this ghastly hotel room that reeked of body odor and old urine, Jose Medina walked in and yelled out two names: Jose Franco and Alejandro Cortez. A dark, slender man with broad shoulders and a teenage mustache stood up with me and brushed off his hands on his already filthy jeans. I had previously overheard him telling another *pollo* he was going to Chicago to make money to send home to his parents and five younger siblings, who were down to surviving on handouts from already strapped relatives. His father had undertaken the same route when his meager farm earnings could no longer sustain the growing family. Unfortunately, he was never heard from again and in all likelihood was one of the many who perish along the way without being identified, buried in hundreds of nameless graves on both sides of the border.

We picked up our tricky bags and silently followed Jose to a minivan, where at least ten other *pollos* and guides were crowding into the backseats. We were heading toward Zaragoza, a dusty village on the outskirts of Juarez teeming with cheap hotels and rowdy bars. A few miles before the village, we stopped at a location known as *la curva,* where the river bends and obscures the view from the opposite shore. I knew this spot well. U.S. border agents aggressively patrolled the American side nightly, arresting as many smugglers and their payloads as they were able to apprehend. Of course, many others took advantage of the agents being busy, and bolted, like drivers speeding past a cop writing a ticket on the shoulder of the highway for someone else. Bandits on the Mexican side preyed on immigrants foolhardy enough to cross the river unescorted by coyotes. Smugglers were known to conspire with these petty thieves, pointing out targets they suspected of having lots of cash or valuables.

Everyone but Alejandro and me was instructed to get out of the van. Jose was the head coyote in the group and was taking special care of us. He explained that we were breaking into smaller groups to attract less attention. The van continued a few hundred yards farther before pulling behind some tall bushes. Jose, Alejandro, and I got out there as the minivan sped off with its lights still extinguished.

The night air hit me with a cold blast after the cramped, humid van. The desert temperature was close to 32 degrees. We slowly made our way to the river and stripped down to our underwear. We tied our street clothes into our tricky bags and held them above our heads. My gun was safe, rolled in my jeans. Then we followed Jose Medina into the frigid Rio Grande.

Summoning all my strength, I inched forward. I was in great physical shape, but still I was barely a match for the river's pull. I did not know much about Alejandro's stamina, but he appeared to be holding his own. We completed the crossing in about ten long minutes.

I could see a green U.S. Border Patrol vehicle in the distance, but we were behind a levee and it was facing in the wrong direction to see us. Our coyote knew his job well.

Jose didn't need any time to recover. I was hoping for a few minutes to catch my breath, but Jose walked over and gave me a rough nudge on the cheek with his foot. My hatred for him was growing by the minute.

"Put your clothes on," he ordered.

I had been so focused on staying alive that I had forgotten how cold it was, until I realized I was shivering. I dressed as fast as I could and joined Jose and Alejandro.

"Let's go before the Border Patrol turns around," Jose directed Alejandro and me in a hushed voice.

Following his lead, we darted away from the river toward the lights of El Paso, first traversing the dangerous stretch of road known as the Border Highway. Besides being heavily patrolled, the four-lane interstate has had a sobering number of pedestrian deaths—immigrants who had managed to cross the Rio Grande but not the highway.

It had been three days since my initial contact with Jose Medina. I had waited in a Mexican fleabag hotel, crossed a frigid, fast-running river, and jumped an interstate highway to cover a distance of less than one mile, a twenty-minute walk under normal conditions. I had traveled such a short distance that I could still see the illuminated billboards of Juarez on the other side of the river as we reached the Medina drop house.

The tiny ranch was right along the highway, separated by only a fence of stone and chain link wire. Jose ordered us to jump over it into the backyard. We entered 5500 Flower Drive through a porch door with the light on in the back. It was 4 A.M. according to the wall clock in the kitchen. Guadalupe Medina, Jose's mother and the family matriarch, was waiting for us in the kitchen by the stove, boiling a pot of beans. She grunted a greeting. She was chunky, rough for her fifty-eight years. Her straight brown hair was pulled back in a clip; her loose long skirt fell below her knees. When I asked her for something to eat, she refused me.

"We eat once a day and you are too late. You will wait until tomorrow to be fed," she coldly informed me.

Besides Alejandro and me, thirteen other immigrants were waiting for passage to Chicago. We all stayed in one bedroom, but it had no furniture. Almost everyone was asleep when we entered, crowded on the cement floor. Through the low light streaming through a small window with an aluminum foil shade, I saw a teenage girl with long black hair lying in a fetal position. She was dressed in jeans and a dark-colored sweater, staring straight ahead, not trying to take advantage of the darkness to sleep.

"What's wrong with her?" I whispered to a woman who identified herself as Consuelo Marquez. "She was raped before we crossed yesterday," she whispered back. "She has not eaten or said a word since we arrived at this house." The girl had been part of Consuelo's group, which was led across the river the day before. The fourteen-year-old had no relatives traveling with her. While at the river, Jose and another smuggler had singled out her and another young girl, convincing them that they did not have to cross the river but could cross at the International Bridge instead. The two smugglers attempted to take one of Consuelo's daughters, but she told them that her family would not be separated. They would cross together or not at all.

Consuelo was traveling with her five children: eight-year-old Jose Pedro, six-year-old Fabiola, and her three teenage daughters, Hermelinda, Elia, and Brinda. Brinda's new husband, Raul, was also with them. Pedro Marquez, Consuelo's husband, had hired the Medinas for several thousand dollars for the seven of them. They had traveled more than twenty-four hours by bus from Jeres, Zacatecas, to get to Juarez. During the bus ride they had heard stories about smugglers taking advantage of immigrants along the border and U.S. agents beating up on the *pollos* coming across.

After they arrived at El Correo Hotel, Consuelo told the person at the desk that they were going to Chicago. She and her family were escorted to a hotel room and instructed to wait for Jose Medina for the crossing. Everything had gone according to plan, except for the disturbing separation of the two young girls at the river. Around midnight, only one of the girls showed up at the Medina drop house in El Paso; she was disheveled and crying. She told Consuelo that she had been raped. The second girl was not part of the group going to Chicago, so she had been brought to the stash house but was immediately sent somewhere else. Jose Medina was later heard bragging about his conquest to several other men. Unfortunately, I was not in a position to investigate the allegation, but if it turned out to be true, I promised myself the scum would pay dearly. It pained me so much to see this young and vulnerable child suffering the way she was, probably wishing she had her mother or father to hold her and tell her everything was going to be okay. This bastard had violated her vulnerability, her belief in the goodness of humankind, and there was nothing I wanted more at that moment than to walk into the next room and beat the total living shit out of him.

Consuelo propped the heads of her two youngest children on tricky bags. She dressed them in their Sunday best for the big trek north. The boy was curled up next to his older sister Hermelinda. He wore a full suit and bow tie, and Fabiola had on a frilly pink dress. These would be their outfits for when they were united with their waiting relatives in Chicago.

Other family groups were also traveling north. Three cousins in their twenties from a small village south of Chihuahua were restlessly using each other for pillows. One had crossed twice in the past but had been deported both times. The other two were making their maiden voyage.

All of us were anxious to get under way, but our Medina coyotes were in charge. And as the days passed, the morning's bean soup seemed to get more and more watery.

The Border Patrol still posed problems, even though we were in Texas. Every morning, a smuggler left 5500 Flower Drive to reconnoiter an immigration checkpoint nearby. The station was manned sporadically, and our guide needed it unmanned to proceed. The circulating rumor was that our address was being staked out by agents, which increased the tension. In fact, the rumor was true. Every so often, I peeked out a window and caught sight of the agents' car parked almost a block away in the shade. I figured they were not raiding the house but only watching it, because they knew I was on an undercover mission and they were my backup. Gary and I had finely tweaked the plan and solidified our signals ahead of my departure for Juarez.

The day before I went undercover, we had met with our counterparts from the Border Patrol's Anti-Smuggling Unit in El Paso. We briefed them on the entire operation and reviewed what to do if I needed assistance or backup. The agents were already savvy to the Medina family. They had even identified some of the safe house operators, knew where the movers stashed their loads of immigrants and narcotics, and had other details about their operation. We were so confident that everything was under control in El Paso that Gary had stayed in Chicago to coordinate the takedown.

Unbeknownst to me, personal conflicts at the El Paso Border Patrol office had interfered with shared intelligence, and there was no backup. Either way, the very presence of the agents was delaying our trip.

Activity around the house really picked up on the third day. The smugglers were as anxious as we were to get going. Their operation depended on quick turnovers in El Paso. Their clients were backlogging in Juarez, and the Medinas were afraid of losing business to competitors.

My heart sank when our transportation finally arrived. A large rented U-Haul truck, parked in front of the house, was to take us to Chicago. From the cargo hold, in which we would be traveling, I wouldn't be able to tell where we were going or what was happening outside. Everyone would be at the mercy of our driver, Gonzalo Manzano. An illegal immigrant himself, he was a faithful employee of the Medinas. He acted like a real badass with the illegal immigrants. He appeared to be in his early twenties and was in dire need of a shave. The points of his cowboy boots stuck out from the bottoms of his beat-up jeans.

I couldn't see his eyes behind a pair of dark aviator sunglasses, but his ugly mood was clear. Guadalupe Medina was urgently directing us to assemble in the front doorway, ready to move. She knew that with agents watching the house, the U-Haul would alert them, so she was trying to ship us when there was a lull in the surveillance. It didn't matter to her if we returned to Mexico or went to Chicago, she just wanted us out. Around lunchtime, Gonzalo backed the truck into the driveway and we began to load.

Gonzalo placed a long board from the truck's loading platform to the ground. The rape victim, still traumatized, was helped up the board by other *pollos,* and they all settled into the cargo compartment. I wanted to be able to identify the smugglers, so I stalled before moving toward the truck, making visual snapshots of the coyotes. This did not sit well with one of the smugglers. Annoyed and aggressive, he pushed me up the plank and yelled, "What the hell are you doing? Get your ass in there, and don't look around!" I lost my balance and struck my head on the edge of the platform, momentarily stunned.

I crawled into the back with a deep pain shooting through my neck. Gonzalo aimed a kick at the last *pollo,* but missed, connecting with the truck instead. I took satisfaction in the small payback for his cruelty, watching him jump up and down in pain. He had to tear a hole in the toe of his boot to relieve the pressure from the swelling.

One woman from our group who refused to sit in the cargo hold was abandoned to fend for herself, and we were finally under way, fourteen paying customers and Gonzalo, our driver. A decoy unit sent out a few minutes before came back to inform us that vehicle spot checks were down, and we were given our final clearance. The back gate was pulled down and locked, and we departed for Chicago.

For a long time, we rode in silence, thinking any noise meant we'd be discovered. The ride was bumpy, and we were all trying to find comfortable positions, knowing we'd be in this dark hole for at least three or four days. The smugglers had not given us food or water. Señora Medina had even confiscated a wheel of cheese, brought all the way from Zacatecas by the Marquezes to give to Pedro in Chicago. The lump where I had hit my head was large and painful, adding to my misery. Eventually it would require surgery, but there was nothing I could do to ease the pain at the moment.

My eyes slowly adjusted to the darkness, and I saw the teenage girl sitting near me, still in distress. When I tried to comfort her, she pulled away from me in fear. She stared at me without responding.

"Everything is going to be okay," I assured her. "Your relatives in Chicago will take care of you." I rolled up my tricky bag and placed it under her neck. She closed her eyes and seemed to feel safe for the first time. But I was filled with anxiety. I prayed we would reach our destination without anyone getting hurt.

I admired the courage of my fellow travelers, especially the exceptionally brave six-year-old Fabiola and her eight-year-old brother, Jose Pedro. Despite the hardships, they were polite and obedient. They held child-sized sombreros, souvenirs of their homeland, in their laps. No one complained. The U-Haul was filled with dreams about a new beginning in Chicago. I hoped and prayed that when the journey was over, some of these desperate, humble people, whose crime was to cross into our country without documentation, would find legal ways to stay. Ultimately they would be granted amnesty under the Immigration Reform and Control Act (IRCA) in 1986, but the fact that I was going to have to arrest them after the takedown was not easy to think about.

Three hours after being on the road, the truck came to an abrupt stop, started backing up, and came to a stop again. Gonzalo pulled open the U-Haul's sliding door and let in the blinding sunlight. When our eyes adjusted, we were dumbfounded to see that we were back at 5500 Flower Drive. Guadalupe Medina was running toward us at full speed, screaming at Gonzalo. "What the hell happened?" she cursed.

"Jose just called saying they had gone through a checkpoint, but he didn't know where you were. You don't have the balls to drive!"

"We couldn't have made it through," Gonzalo explained meekly. "We'll have to try again tomorrow."

Guadalupe continued screaming at her driver, ignoring the passengers in the hold. I took the opportunity to step forward.

"Señora Guadalupe," I said calmly, "your chauffeur is gutless, but I am willing to drive to Chicago without pay. I have nothing to lose. Please give me a chance."

"You see, Gonzalo?" Señora Medina snapped, glaring in his face. "Even this ignorant *pollo* can do better than you. He will help you drive when you take off again." With that, she stormed back to the house.

Gonzalo was livid. "I'll deal with you later," he threatened, but I was equally hard-ass.

"You know where to find me," I shot back.

I knew the Medinas were partial to their driver, and I was expendable. But I had to pursue my chance to be in the cab. Jose Rodriguez, the scout car driver, returned to the house with a couple of cases of beer for the coyotes, and the cargo of *pollos* was once again herded into a bedroom. Another load had arrived since our false start, so space was at a premium.

Everyone was as pleasant as possible. My group, in admiration of me now that I had stood my ground against Gonzalo, gave me approving glances. Many of us stayed awake talking about our journeys to this point and our hopes for the future. Consuelo's story was as memorable as it was courageous.

Pedro Marquez, her husband, had started crossing into the United States during the Bracero program, back when braceros, unskilled farm laborers, were allowed to enter the country and work seasonal crops along the southwest border before returning to Mexico at the end of the harvest. In 1964, the Bracero program was terminated. Pedro, like many other Mexicans, stayed in our country illegally because crossing the border before and after harvests became prohibitively expensive and dangerous. Eventually he moved north to Chicago and landed a job cleaning out cargo cars for a train company.

He sent remittances to Consuelo for their nine children in Mexico. When his oldest daughter, Irma, was diagnosed with a heart disease and told her life expectancy was eighteen years, Consuelo and Irma crossed into the United States, aided by smugglers. After Irma's condition stabilized, Consuelo returned to Zacatecas and her other children, who had remained with relatives.

Pedro and Consuelo didn't want the family to be separated, so Consuelo was bringing everyone left to Chicago. They also knew it was only a matter of time before their children would want to venture north to escape the dire poverty they lived in, with few educational opportunities and even less of a chance of ever making a decent living. Pedro had not been able to locate the same smugglers his wife and daughter had used for their first journey, so he asked for a referral from other newly arrived Mexicans. The Medina name kept coming up, and Pedro decided to call them.

He made contact with Jose and was assured that his family would be well cared for. Safety was important to Pedro. In addition to his wife, four of his daughters would be traveling, and he had heard of smugglers who abused females. He wanted smugglers who were trustworthy, if such men existed.

The Medinas weren't to be trusted. I felt like I was now carrying the responsibility for the safety of everyone in our group.

The next morning, I found Guadalupe Medina alone in the kitchen preparing the bean soup for the day. She was far from pleased to have two loads, twice as many mouths to feed. "Buenos días," I said to her in greeting with a disarmingly soft tone. "It smells good in here. Can I help you with what you are doing?"

She asked me to wash bowls, welcoming the chance to have someone new to complain to. As I cleaned the dishes, she explained the dilemma with Gonzalo. "He has been working for us for a long time and I know his family," she said. "He lacks guts, but he is loyal and I cannot choose you over him to drive."

"That's okay, I just want to help," I answered. "I do not want his job. I just want to get to Chicago safely and quickly." I did not want to look suspiciously eager. I knew Gonzalo was more likely to seek my assistance on his terms.

After washing the grime from the pots and pans, I returned to my group in the bedroom to wait for our second stab at departure. Soon checkpoint scouts began hollering and directing us back into the U-Haul to take advantage of another window of opportunity. I picked up four one-gallon containers of water from the kitchen without asking anyone's permission and passed them to my fellow passengers. I brazenly asked Gonzalo if I should join him in the cab. He responded with a shove so hard that I found myself in the bay of the U-Haul unaided by the plank. I took a position near the tailgate to overhear any last-minute instructions between the Medinas and their driver.

I wasn't as anxious as I had been the previous day. Again we all arranged ourselves in our positions. Being in the back of a windowless truck was aggravating, especially when our prior journey had been three hours of getting nowhere. We had to rely on faith that we were advancing this time. Gonzalo seemed to be taking a local route. The truck jerked into and out of stops and starts every few minutes, suggesting traffic lights and heavy congestion. I later overheard that he had gotten lost in El Paso trying to shake possible Border Patrol agents, and he had wasted two hours getting back to Interstate 10 before heading to New Mexico.

After three or four hours of smooth travel, Gonzalo brought the U-Haul to another abrupt stop. With a loud screech, he yanked up the tail door and looked straight at me. We were on a rural stretch of road in the middle of nowhere. I positioned myself so I could reach my .25-caliber pistol if I needed it.

"Get out!" he ordered me. I wasn't sure what to expect. "It's your turn to drive," he growled, much to my relief. He motioned for me to follow him. I jumped to the ground before he slammed the gate shut one more time. After I had entered the driver's side of the cab and he had settled in as the passenger, I asked him where we were and which direction we were going. Once again we were lost. He had taken a wrong road somewhere and we had to figure out our bearings.

"No problem," I told him as I started up the engine. I knew the area, but Gonzalo was under the impression my sense of direction was good luck.

Unfortunately, we were still on the wrong side of a border checkpoint near Alamogordo, New Mexico. Approaching the post, I saw agents setting up traffic cones, only minutes away from beginning vehicle stops. I proceeded cautiously past them without being stopped. As before, I thought my fellow agents were dutifully protecting me while following the progress of my case.

I felt more in control now that I was driving the truck. I was in the middle of a fantasy about pulling into a roadside diner and pigging out, recovering some of the ten pounds I had lost in the last three days, when I spotted the flashing lights of a New Mexico State Police vehicle in my rearview mirror.

"We are fucked," Gonzalo said, thankful he wasn't driving. "Tell them I am only a passenger and I will make sure you can drive for us again," he said to bribe me. "If you mention Señora Medina, her sons will come after you."

I knew I had to do business with the officer outside the truck, so I jumped out and began to approach his cruiser. I assumed that either he wasn't aware he had interrupted my undercover operation, or he *was* aware and was looking for a discreet update.

"Stop where you are! Don't *move*!" the uniformed trooper yelled as I approached. I appreciated what I hoped was play-acting, but I couldn't answer him in English because I was beside the truck within earshot of Gonzalo. My unkempt appearance and dirty smell would certainly not make me look legitimate. I might not have believed me, either.

The officer unsnapped his holster, and I raised my hands in the air so he could see I had nothing threatening. I moved slowly closer to discuss the situation with him in private. In a low voice, I told him I was an INS agent, but he either didn't hear me or didn't believe me.

"Open the back of that U-Haul!" he demanded. When

I didn't respond, he walked toward the gate himself and grabbed the handle.

"You do not want to do that," I warned. He turned back toward me in disbelief, positioning himself defensively with his hand on his gun. The trooper was unaccustomed to Mexicans speaking fluent English, let alone giving orders. He used his walkie-talkie to request backup, keeping his gaze dead on me.

I decided my best bet was to crawl into the backseat of the squad car, leaving my door open. The trooper slammed it closed before pulling himself into the front seat. As he picked up his radio to contact his dispatcher, I addressed him by the name I read on his badge. "Officer Skinner, I am a federal agent engaged in an undercover operation, and we have a load of immigrants in the back of that truck. This is a legitimate operation and I need to ask that you allow us to proceed."

"If you are an agent, can you explain why there is an APB on your truck, issued in El Paso?" he inquired.

I was completely caught off guard. I had assumed that the El Paso Border Patrol had judiciously given us clearance, and I now realized with a sinking feeling that this trooper was not part of my protection. I was angry. I was on a dangerous undercover mission and absolutely no one had a clue where I was. Skinner agreed that I had a cargo of immigrants in the U-Haul, but as for my role, he thought I was a dirty, lying coyote spinning a tale to get away. The week before, he told me, another "Mezzzzzican" had tried the same thing during a narcotics stop.

"Dispatch, would you send a backup to assist with a load of immigrants and one suspect already in custody?" I heard him project through the radio's static. He began filling out his report, recording the time and circumstances of the traffic stop in his log.

"Officer Skinner," I continued, "if I were a real criminal, I could have put a hole in the back of your head." I wasn't comfortable making him feel so vulnerable, but I was running low on options. He had neglected to pat me down, standard protocol for allowing a suspect to enter a squad car.

I handed him my small pistol as a gesture of good faith and promised him that a single phone call would prove my story. Skinner again radioed his dispatcher, to postpone backup, and relayed the phone number I had pulled from my wallet, a contact from the El Paso sector. To my shock, that bastard had given me a nonworking number and the call was unsuccessful. I offered another contact, a dispatcher at the Border Patrol headquarters who might or might not remember my name and identity. This time it worked, and Officer Skinner gave my weapon back and opened my door without saying a word. What an asshole: he could at least have said good luck. I know I would have had I run in to an undercover agent on such a dangerous mission.

Although I was incredibly relieved, I still had the task of explaining the whole thing to Gonzalo. I returned to my driver's seat trying to think of a believable story. Gonzalo had been following my actions in disbelief through the rearview mirror. I took my place behind the wheel and drove off without a word. When he was certain we weren't going to be pulled over again, he asked me bluntly what had happened.

"It was easy," I said. "I gave him my last hundred-dollar bill and I expect you to repay me when we get to Chicago." Gonzalo muttered that he thought crooked cops were only in

Mexico and laughed off his debt to me with a "yeah, right." For the next hour, we rode in silence.

We pulled into a rest stop in Tularosa, New Mexico, to change drivers and refuel. I pumped gas while Gonzalo went inside the store. During his absence I checked on the passengers in the cargo hold. They were hungry but otherwise comfortable, and I promised them I would somehow get food to them after dark. Making them travel all the way to Chicago under such deplorable conditions was extremely difficult for me. I genuinely liked them. The coyotes and their bosses were the ones I was after, yet I had to remember that the *pollos* were breaking the law, too. I tried to focus on the fact that I would look out for their well-being as best I could until Chicago.

Gonzalo emerged from the convenience store with a six-pack of beer and chips and took over the driving. We lumbered along, with me liberally drinking the beers I pulled from the plastic rings. I was a co-driver now, and I didn't want him driving after six beers, I reasoned.

I dozed and woke often over the next few hours, as Gonzalo assured me he was not in need of relief. Hours into the night, I woke up to snow pellets hitting the windshield. A sign illuminated by the truck's headlights indicated we were one hundred miles away from Amarillo, Texas. It was three in the morning, we had been on the road at least fifteen hours, and we still hadn't reached Amarillo. I was warm enough in the cab, but the cargo hold was not heated.

"*¿Dónde estamos?*" I asked Gonzalo.

His blank response told me everything. The snow picked up until we were driving in whiteout conditions, low on fuel, and lost. Gonzalo said he had gotten off I-40 to look for a rest area and had kept to the back roads thinking they would have better services. I played with the radio and learned we were in the middle of the worst snowstorm in fifty years. I took over the driving, and just as I was imagining the U-Haul filled with innocent people falling into a ditch in the blizzard and running out of gas, we came upon a country store in the middle of nowhere.

To my utter amazement, it was open for business, confirmed by lights we could barely make out through the blowing snow. I told Gonzalo we needed to let our passengers warm up inside, but he was without compassion.

"Fuck them," he mumbled. "Find out where we are, get gas, and let's go!"

I pulled up to the old fuel pumps and let Gonzalo handle the gas transaction while I slipped inside and purchased four blankets from a small pile of bedcovers the store had for sale. I threw them quickly into the back of the truck, not wanting the blowing snow to invade what little warmth had been created by the passengers' body temperatures. The group was cold, exhausted, and in extreme discomfort. They had been bouncing around without cushioning or heat for two days. The temperature in the cargo hold was barely warmer than outside, and it was 22 degrees outside.

Alejandro and another young man were propped up toward the gate, the coldest part of the truck, knowing they were in better shape. They all suffered the journey through needlessly inhumane conditions. They had not stretched or been given access to a bathroom. They had not been allowed to leave the truck under any circumstances and had resorted to using empty water jugs to relieve themselves. They had been wearing all the clothing they had been carrying to stay warm.

I stayed on as the driver and managed to get us back to I-40, helped by directions I received in the store. Slowly, the storm eased off and the conditions improved. The U-Haul plodded toward Oklahoma with Gonzalo snoring away.

By daybreak we were nearing Oklahoma City via the Oklahoma Turnpike. For a stretch we were followed for thirty minutes by a marked Border Patrol cruiser, who began tailing us at a tollbooth, but he never intercepted us and eventually peeled away. When we finally passed Tulsa, I wanted to begin planning an endgame with Gary, but I needed a pay phone. Gonzalo refused to let me out of the truck to make a call or check on the passengers in the hold. He chuckled as he callously told me, "What difference does it make if someone back there is dead? There is nothing you can do." I was disgusted to the core by the cowardly worm, but logically, I couldn't mutiny. I would be putting the lives of everyone in the load in danger. He'd get his due at the takedown.

Several hours later we pulled into a gas station just north of Springfield, Missouri. I ran for the restroom without waiting for Gonzalo's permission. Secured in a stall, I used a paper napkin I had grabbed from the food counter at the last stop and a pencil in my pocket to scribble my home telephone number and a message for my wife, who was almost certain to be home because of our two young sons:

Terrie, we are in Missouri. Please tell Gary we will arrive around midnight on November 21st at the Standard station in Joliet where we took down the Arizona case. We can take the load down right there.

Keeping an eye out for Gonzalo, I waited until the clerk at the counter was alone. I whispered to him that I was a federal agent and I needed his help. I gave him the note, begging him to pass the message to my wife. He didn't believe me, especially in light of my disheveled appearance and rank odor.

The clerk threatened to call the police, but nonetheless, cued by the desperation in my stare, he hid my note from view when Gonzalo approached. Whether he made the call or not was now beyond my control.

I got back to the U-Haul ahead of Gonzalo and claimed the driver's seat. Being behind the wheel was essential to my plan, even if Gary did not receive the call with my instructions. If I didn't take charge now, I would end up at the Medinas' Chicago safe house without backup. I knew Terrie must be sick with worry about my condition and whereabouts. She always was when I went undercover and she hadn't heard from me in several days.

The road through Missouri seemed to go on forever. Gonzalo dozed off and on, occasionally offering to drive. During a rare conversation between us, he told me he planned to keep the young girl a day or two, having his way with her before she called her relatives. He was taken aback when I told him that no such plan was going to happen. Our power struggle was intensifying, but I was sick of the pig and could no longer take it. We crossed the state line into Illinois at nightfall. The passengers in the cargo hold had spent close to thirty-six torturous hours without food, exercise, services, or water beyond the four gallons I had stowed for us in El Paso. I pulled the U-Haul into a service station with a diner at a freeway exit, told Gonzalo to refuel, and placed a takeout order with the three-hundred-pound cook flipping patties at the grill. "I want nineteen hamburgers with fries, seventeen hot chocolates, and two coffees to go," I announced.

I didn't care what Gonzalo thought. I returned to the truck, pulled open the hatch, and distributed the meals. Everyone seemed to be in an acceptable medical condition, except for one man with frostbite. However, even he wanted to continue to Chicago without further medical attention. I invited anyone who wanted to stretch their legs to walk around outside, but no one accepted, too scared of being reported or abandoned. They graciously took the food and insisted we keep driving, especially when I told them we were only a few hours from Chicago.

Gonzalo surprised me when he ordered the young lady to get out of the hold and into the cab. The girl, squeezed between Gonzalo and me, was thoroughly terrified of us both. She did not respond to any of Gonzalo's crass overtures, and when he grabbed her chin to make her look at him, I demanded that he stop. Thankfully, he obliged and did not bother her again.

We continued our journey in silence, the time passing slower and slower the closer we got to our destination. I had estimated our arrival time perfectly. At ten minutes before midnight, we approached the exit leading to the Standard station, where hopefully Gary was waiting with a backup team. We had used the gas station before, taking down an Arizona case in which smugglers had transported a cargo of Mexicans in a motor home. The station had served us well then, and I was anxiously anticipating a similar outcome now.

As I slowed down to exit, Gonzalo grew agitated. "Just keep going," he demanded. "We can easily make it to Chicago with the fuel we have." I continued to the service station anyway, and parked the U-Haul away from the gas pumps. Gonzalo was becoming suspicious.

I pulled the keys from the ignition and went inside the station, not knowing what to expect. To my delight, Gary and several other agents were there waiting for us. The restaurant clerk at the diner had called my wife, and she in turn had contacted Gary. Gary, the other agents, and I now quickly finalized the details of the rest of our mission, and I returned to the truck, newly energized.

"Get out!" I ordered Gonzalo.

Without hesitation, Gonzalo leapt out of the truck, fists up. I gave him a straight cut to the jaw, causing him to fall to the pavement. When he got up, I successfully stomped on his injured toe. He was howling as I put him under arrest. The young lady in the cab was overwhelmed with disbelief. With law enforcement on the scene, her already horrific journey was ending in another nightmare. I tried to reassure her, but from her point of view, I was now her enemy. Even though our undercover operation was going to have us continue in the U-Haul to the Medinas' Chicago clearinghouse, I gently removed her from the truck and placed her in an agent's car, hopefully sparing her additional trauma.

We searched Gonzalo and found a small book with many of the Medinas' telephone numbers, including a local Chicago number. I dialed it from the pay phone in the Standard station, hoping to reach someone at the safe house.

"Where the hell have you guys been and where the hell is Gonzalo?" inquired the angry man on the other end. I explained that we were in danger of being caught, that Gonzalo was busy with the cargo, and that I was a co-driver and needed the address and directions fast; policemen were all over the area. He complied and said we would need about an hour to get there from where we were, and to be sure we weren't being followed.

Gary and I decided to keep the sting a secret from the cargo passengers. I pulled open the gate under the pretense of telling them we were only an hour away, and no one seemed aware of any of the commotion that had taken place with Gonzalo. They were patient and composed, waiting for their final leg to end.

The drive to the clearinghouse address seemed to take no time at all. I soon found myself in an alley on the south side of Chicago. I had a walkie-talkie now so I would be able to communicate with Gary and the team. The man who had answered the phone had told me the apartment was on the second floor of a three-story building, and I was to come through the alley to the rear door. Because of the late hour, no one was out on the streets of the dreary neighborhood, and the graffiti-riddled gates of the storefronts were closed and locked.

Knocking on the back door of the second-floor apartment, I was met by a middle-aged Mexican man with a thick mustache and a beer belly protruding from a dirty white T-shirt. He was the same man who had answered the phone.

"¿Dónde está Gonzalo?" he asked again.

The back door of the U-Haul had been pulled up to allow the passengers to follow me. I told them to wait a few minutes so I could get to the apartment and have the door opened before they joined me. As instructed, they started arriving, and the head honcho had no choice but to let us in. Collecting smuggling fees and efficiently moving people to their relatives was now his priority, but the situation remained extremely tense. The other smugglers in the house were not comfortable that Gonzalo was missing.

I was less worried that they would suspect I was a federal agent than that they would think I was a smuggler from a competing syndicate, trying to steal their payload. Before the situation could escalate, I pulled the gun given to me by an agent at the gas station and screamed for everyone to freeze. "You're all under arrest! Get on the floor!" I commanded. If my appearance was not official, my weapon made it so. I summoned my backup officers, who were waiting in the shadows of the alley.

We herded all the people who had traveled with me more than 1,500 miles, from the desert in El Paso to the dark alleys of south Chicago, back into the U-Haul so we could transport them to the federal building downtown for processing. I had witnessed their suffering firsthand from a perspective no other U.S. immigration agent had ever experienced, and their plight had a strong impact on me. It was not a great feeling knowing that everyone in the load was going to be detained, but the law was the law. Poverty and desperation drove these otherwise decent people to violate legal U.S. immigration policy, which I was sworn to uphold. That did not make my position much easier for me. All of the immigrants, who were now witnesses, were terrified and confused. The man with frostbite had to be hospitalized on account of his medical condition.

A total of four smugglers were arrested that night. We obtained warrants for six others in El Paso, including Jose and

Guadalupe Medina. Unfortunately, Jose Medina was not at the El Paso house when agents served the warrants, and he was not apprehended. Rumors circulated that he knew about the warrant and had fled to Mexico. I was going to have to be patient, but I had no doubt the bastard and I would meet again.

Throughout the undercover mission, I knew that my rights were protected by the U.S. Constitution, and that when the job was done I would return home to the comfort of my wife and family. My life might have been in danger, but my freedom in the United States was secure. The *pollos,* on the other hand, were leaving their homeland for a world completely unknown. They risked exploitation, victimization, deportation, and even their lives at every turn. They were illegal and vulnerable, always in jeopardy, living in fear in the land of their dreams. The Rio Grande flowed between their desperate poverty and their cautious hope. The problem, however, was that their sojourns in the United States were against the law.

The ordeal from the border to Chicago had been harrowing for all of us. My oath to enforce the law and all its responsibilities had been ingrained in me from the very first day of my twelve weeks of training at the U.S. Border Patrol Academy. An equally important lesson was to always keep our emotions in check. There was no gray area here: if we did not uphold the law, we were not fulfilling our oath. In spite of the harsh conditions and maltreatment I had witnessed during our journey north, my fellow passengers had broken the law and entered our country illegally. They had joined in a conspiracy with criminal defendants to be smuggled to Chicago. From the beginning of the case to its finality, there was no doubt in my mind what I needed to do and what I would do: arrest everyone.

There is no room for emotion during these critical points in an undercover case. Showing weakness or hesitation during a takedown could make for a volatile situation. The safety of everyone, from the agents to the victims to the witnesses to the criminals, is the top priority. But that didn't mean that I was immune to the plight of others.

My ability to remain stoic and in control during an assignment came from having methodically thought out a situation and considered all the possibilities, from its beginning to any and all possible conclusions. I had reviewed my role in the Juarez to Chicago assignment in my mind a great many times.

After a raid or a takedown, I always had a period of emotional reflection. I was human, after all. I'd often meet with my fellow agents. Our inflated egos needed boosting and we loved meeting at a bar where other agents were ready to glowingly receive us with pats on the back. My comrades and I could commiserate in a supportive group about the emotional difficulties of our job. Working in human smuggling was different than working in drug smuggling. We couldn't just tag the evidence and shelve it to complete the assignment. A case needed to be built and defendants had to be prosecuted. Our range of emotions was extreme; there were highs and lows, with no in between. I thought of myself as the nicest guy in the world, but when I worked those cases I was a hardened agent.

Consuelo and her children hadn't believed my reassurance that they were going to be released on their own recognizance, so they were pleasantly surprised when Pedro picked them up at Chicago's U.S. immigration office. They had agreed to testify against the Medinas and, in fact, were interviewed numerous times by federal agents and assistant U.S. attorneys.

The immigrants were the commodity. They had been smuggled in, and in turn, they were the best witnesses to describe all the events and people involved in their illegal entry. In defending themselves, defendants have a right to confront their accusers.

Our two options were to keep the witnesses locked up until the case was over and then deport them from the United States, or to allow them to post a bond and be released. The first option would quickly fill up all our jail space; thus in most cases the immigrant witnesses were released on a recognizance bond, as long as they agreed to present themselves when called to testify. They were not considered a threat in the community and not likely to abscond.

Although all of the passengers in our case presented themselves during court proceedings against the smugglers, ultimately only Consuelo testified. The others had their cases handled by the agency's Deportation Branch. They were given eighteen- to twenty-four-month permits, which included the authorization to work legally in the United States if they were older than eighteen. In the end they were instructed to voluntarily return to Mexico or their native countries. I often wondered how many did in fact return.

Gonzalo, Guadalupe, and the others arrested later pled guilty to smuggling charges. Manzano and Señora Medina were each sentenced to three years on two felony counts and two-thousand-dollar fines. However, their sentences were suspended. Manzano was deported to Mexico, and Guadalupe Medina, an American citizen, returned to El Paso.

Gary and I were frustrated that the length and danger of my undercover mission had produced a bonanza of criminal smugglers but with minimal impact on the big picture. Ten smugglers was a coup for the agency. The problem was that immigrant smuggling sentences were not nearly as severe as we would have liked, probably not even harsh enough to deter those just busted from returning to the smuggling trade as soon as they were out. In light of the absolutely subhuman treatment of most immigrants in transit, like what I had just witnessed, this was a travesty. However, that reality in no way diminished our satisfaction in the success of our mission. We had put the lowlife Medinas on high notice that they were not as untouchable as they might have believed.

CHAPTER TWO

On the Border: The Beginning

REMARKABLY, THE MIGRANT'S journey I had undertaken during my Juarez mission is repeated thousands of times every day along our borders. No matter how high the new border fence, how expensive the fees for a coyote, or how vigilant the U.S. border agents, desperation outweighs the risk for these people. When we throw more government resources at the Mexican border, coyotes resort to using more dangerous methods and routes. Though the numbers are inexact regarding immigrant deaths from heat exposure and dehydration in the desert, and from drownings in the Rio Grande, they are significant and tragic.

A coyote-guided trek across the parched, inhospitable Southwest is considered to be the most economical crossing, but it takes fifteen to thirty hours and costs more than a thousand dollars a person. The temperatures are easily in excess of 110 degrees during the day and below freezing at night in wintertime.

If a vehicle is used to get across the border, the smuggling fees spike three- or four-fold. Some immigrants pay to cross straight up at a point of entry, using counterfeit documents or, in many cases, hidden inside the vehicle. In at least one case, an immigrant was sewn into the backseat of a van. Many have also been found riding on top of the motor under the hood. Others have been discovered hidden inside the dashboard and even hanging on to the undercarriage. Smugglers also take illegal immigrants jammed into cars across the roughest, least patrolled sections of the desert, or they pack them in after they pick them up from arranged fields or drop houses. Sadly, deaths and injuries in accidents involving these overloaded vehicles are on the rise, with or without law enforcement being in hot pursuit. Smugglers and their drivers routinely crash their vehicles into fences along the road, totally disregarding the life-and-limb consequences to their passengers, when they try evasive maneuvers.

While Mexicans provide the migrant stereotype, people of all races and cultures pay enormous fees and risk their lives every day for the chance to start a new life in the United States. Central and South Americans sometimes pay between $7,000 and $10,000 for passage in cargo holds of unseaworthy boats. Middle Eastern, Pakistani, and Chinese immigrants pay upwards of $30,000 to be smuggled to our country, many of them using well-entrenched and protected trafficking organizations in existence throughout Latin America and the Western Hemisphere. The services of smugglers are used by 80 to 90 percent of hopeful migrants from countries around the world. Only a handful try to make it on their own.

Unlike my undercover crossing which involved coyotes and *pollos* discussing business in a bar at the border, most of today's deals are completed in the traveler's village, using familiar coyote contacts or arranged by relatives already in the United States who have used the smuggling organization before. Coyote-guided crossings are considered safer than going it alone, but they are still high risk, as evidenced by the large number of bodies found each year in the Arizona desert, in boxcars, and throughout Mexico from groups making their way north.

No matter from where they originate, those who are apprehended are immediately deported. More often than not they try to return. In fact, their transport fee typically includes "guaranteed free tries" until they are successful. Ninety-five percent eventually are. They spend their life savings to get to the United States, so they have nothing of monetary value to return home to.

My fellow U-Haul passengers left Mexico because their families were starving and there was no way to make money. Getting across the border was not nearly as life threatening as having no rice or beans. For the Marquez family, the dream was to save enough money to return to Mexico to build a home and raise a family. They had not planned to stay, but Pedro and the children became legal United States citizens as a result of the Immigration Reform and Control Act of 1986. Under that act, more than three million illegal immigrants received amnesty, on the condition that they had been in the United States since before 1982.

Their first couple of years in Chicago were hard. Everyone had to find a job, including fifteen-year-old Brinda. Pedro managed to rent a small two-bedroom apartment in a low-income neighborhood. Sleazy supervisors and managers at the factories exploited them by first charging them a hundred-dollar fee for employment, then firing them after a few weeks so they could exploit someone else.

Today, Pedro and Consuelo's children are economically sound, well-educated, productive, proud Americans. Without a job in the United States, he would not have stayed. The rest of his family would not have come if they, too, had not been able to find work here. Pedro had always intended to return to Mexico, and he and his wife eventually did, to raise cattle.

Enforcement of immigration laws in the interior has always been a low priority. This neglect by our leaders has resulted in the situation we have now—ten to fifteen million illegal immigrants residing in the United States with no easy resolution in sight.

According to public records, the Medina family still owns 5500 Flower Drive. The new border wall, which now runs along the Rio Grande on the El Paso side, can be seen from the kitchen window. However, the wall cannot keep out determined *pollos* who eventually find ways to cross.

Where once the risk to immigrants was primarily the river and border patrol agents on the U.S. side, the drugs wars have upped the danger a hundred-fold. Crossing the border should not be a death sentence. The drug lords are so despicable that migrants without any connection to the drug trade are victims of unthinkable brutality. One drug dynasty, the Zetas cartel, has started a practice of kidnapping large groups of migrants making their way north in order to rob and extort them. They hold them for ransom, forcing them to have their contacts in the United States pay for their release and according to many reports, recruiting them or forcing them to be foot soldiers.

In August 2010, seventy-two migrants from El Salvador, Honduras, Ecuador, and Brazil were found shot to death in an isolated ranch in San Fernando, Mexico, fourteen miles south of Brownsville, Texas. One Mexican marine was killed during a gun battle with gang members at the ranch after a lone survivor alerted a traffic checkpoint guard about the shootings. Three cartel gunmen were also killed. The fifty-eight men and fourteen women were found piled on top of each other, many blindfolded with their hands tied behind their backs. The survivor said the massacre began when some migrants resisted demands for ransom.

Despite assurances by the Mexican government that they had solved the crimes and captured the perpetrators, a few months later authorities found a mass grave with the bodies of 177 more individuals who had been pulled off buses heading north. The burial site was not far from the massacre at the ranch. Even more troubling, the bus companies were so scared of retaliation by the gangs that the kidnappings were not even reported. More than four hundred pieces of their unclaimed luggage sat at the bus station in Matamoros, Tamaulipas, Mexico, right across the Rio Grande from Brownsville.

In April 2011, sixteen local police officers were charged with providing protection to the thugs responsible for the mass murders. They had to be held in protective custody, because the community was so angry. Mexican authorities also arrested dozens of others, the most significant being the ruthless head of Los Zetas, Omar Martin Estrada Luna. Authorities believe Estrada Luna was the mastermind behind both massacres.

Some estimates report that more than 1,600 migrants a month are kidnapped to be gunmen and foot soldiers in the armies of the drug cartels, adding to the unfathomable misery and danger of the journey. The fact that many Mexican police are on the payroll of the gangs makes the kidnappings nearly impossible to report.

I, as much as anybody, am empathetic to the despair of my Mexican neighbors on the shores of the Rio Bravo, as the Rio Grande is known in Mexico. The river divides one of the largest cross-border metropolitan areas in the world, El Paso on the American side and Juarez on the Mexican side. Like the Berlin Wall, which divided one city between two nations, the river flowing through the El Paso–Juarez metropolis separates two cities, two countries, and two worlds.

I know the world of poverty the Mexicans inhabit. The fact that I was lucky enough to be born and raised on the American side of the river doesn't mean I grew up rich or without empathy for the misery of others; in fact, my upbringing was just the opposite. Even so, when I became an agent for the United States Border Patrol I took an oath to uphold the law of our great nation, and crossing the border without authorization or permission is against the law, no matter how justifiable and honorable your intentions might be to yourself.

The Texas borderland is in my blood. I was born in a border town in 1953, the ninth of my parents' fifteen children, delivered in a midwife's house in Presidio, Texas, across the Rio Grande from Ojinaga, Mexico. Pancho Villa, the great warrior horseman of the Mexican Revolution, commanded his rebel army to a decisive battle there in 1913, sending the last of the federalist government troops fleeing across the river into Presidio. After my birth, my mother took me back to the family homestead in Redford.

The six rooms of the simple house already barely accommodated my parents and my eight older brothers and sisters, and though I was the youngest at the time, six more children were yet to come. The house had passed from my grandfather to my father. My grandfather, Facundo Acosta, was a mixture of Apache and Jumano Indian from Chihuahua, northern Mexico, and was one of the early settlers of Redford.

The number of structures on the property changed as the family grew. The original house had been two rooms with a dirt floor, built of adobe. By the time I was born, a second, bigger house had been built, which had cement laid over the adobe to strengthen its walls. Both homes were within seventy-five yards of a regional irrigation canal, which fed water to fields of cotton in the Presidio Plains below.

Because we never had plumbing or running water, we used water transported from a neighbor's well in fifty-five gallon containers for our personal hygiene and household chores. The houses had no electricity until I was six. Before that, we used kerosene lanterns for light.

The large house was built on a small hill that overlooked a fifteen-acre tract of land that included about ten acres of farmable property. One of the tallest pecan trees in town grew behind the smaller house. The tree was a gathering place for many of our friends during the winter months. Everybody had fruit trees along the canal, offering mulberries, pomegranates, and peaches for the picking.

We planted patches of tomatoes, watermelon, chilies, and squash for ourselves and we always kept a small number of cows, goats, and chickens for milk and eggs. Each December one choice fatted pig found itself on our table, in a wonderful family celebration and feast.

The education available to us was second-rate. Our textbooks were castoffs from better school districts and our school building had only three rooms. One room was divided by a removable wooden partition, where first grade and what we called hi-first were taught. A year in hi-first normally followed first grade in our school because most, if not all of us, did not speak English when we reached school age, and we had to go through a second year of English instruction before we were considered ready for second grade. Another room was divided to accommodate the second/third grades and the fourth/fifth grades. My favorite teacher was my second and third grade teacher, Mrs. Lucia Madrid. She was an amazing woman. She established a lending library in our town with her personal collection of ten thousand books, making library cards from the backs of cereal boxes. In a White House ceremony in 1990, she was honored as one of President George W. Bush's Thousand Points of Light and deservedly given the President's Volunteer Action Award and the Ronald Reagan Award for Volunteer Excellence.

Her brother-in-law, Edmundo Madrid, was a wonderful mentor to me as well. He occupied the third room of our school, where he taught grades six, seven, and eight. Mr. Madrid had served in France in the U.S. Army during World War II, and he taught me French from a textbook I bought at a secondhand store in Presidio. Through the tales of his adventures in Europe, he stirred my interest in travel, and I knew one day I also would explore the world. The Madrids also fostered my love of reading.

However inadequate the curriculum may have been, I cherished learning. My mother had not been schooled beyond the fifth grade, and I was determined to make the most of my education.

The school year began in September and ended in early May, when the onions and cantaloupes were ready to be picked. The onions started growing in April in rows upon rows in the massive irrigated fields near Presidio. Everyone who was able in our family worked, and we were paid by the sack. We'd pull as many of the green shoots as we could grab in a handful, then snip the roots and tops with shears before we laid them in a basket. When a basket was filled, we'd empty it in a sack, and when the sack was full, we'd leave it on the row for the supervisor to count and collect, each one weighing about fifty pounds. At the end of the day, a picker earned about four or five dollars—luckily our family had lots of pickers.

Loaders, who threw the sacks onto the truck, were paid more than pickers. The crew chief was paid by the number of sacks picked and loaded by his crew of four. I was a little squirt, but the higher pay appealed to me and at the age of twelve I begged for a chance to be a loader. The bigger guys grabbed their sacks and threw them on the truck bed in one motion. I had to shift a sack onto my knee, then nudge it higher before I could shove it the final distance onto the truck, but I persevered. Every loader was paid the same and I had to pull my weight. I never slacked off for a moment. When our family went home that evening, I lay down on the cement floor and didn't wake up until daybreak, covered in a little blanket my mother had tucked around me.

After picking onions, we picked cantaloupes in May and June. We had to strap the collection bags over our shoulders and bend down to pick them. I couldn't stand up completely, because if I did, the bag might slip and hit the ground, possibly ruining the collected cantaloupes.

After the onions and cantaloupes were harvested, we'd travel farther to harvest other crops. We would go to other towns like Pecos or Muleshoe to harvest cucumbers and cabbage. We'd find cotton to pick anywhere from Muleshoe to Artesia, New Mexico, then farther north in New Mexico toward Portales. We would miss a good portion of the beginning of the school year when we were working the late summer and autumn harvests. We'd drive from place to place in a pickup truck usually belonging to someone overseeing the crew. The sides had holes that could be rigged with poles and tarps to protect our belongings. My mother would ride in the cab of the truck, but at least ten of us would ride in the back with our necessities.

The bigger properties had primitive accommodations with beds for us. Some had little shacks or outbuildings that were lent to the migrants for shelter. The shack in Pecos was ours at ten dollars a week. We would stay there for four to five weeks on our northward trek year after year. We weeded their cotton fields and picked their cantaloupes or onions. The shack was a one-room frame with no insulation, two-by-fours on the inside and cement and plaster on the outside. Upon our arrival, we'd clean it out, mop the floors, dust the three beds, scrub the ancient refrigerator, then neatly unpack our two or three pairs of pants, work shoes, and pots and pans and be settled within two or three hours. Other places had barrack-style housing. Every family would have a little area, but no privacy. We would all share one kitchen, equipped with a few double-burner camping stoves.

My mother would get up by 3 A.M. to prepare lunch for us that we would eat in the fields. The rest of us would get up between 5 A.M. and 5:30 A.M. She'd join us to work all day in the scorching heat and return in the evening to make us supper. She usually made us beans and potatoes, but on weekends after we had been paid, we were treated to delicious meat dishes, such as chili con carne. My mother was a wonderful cook and never failed to serve us a pile of steaming tortillas at every meal.

We lived with a community sensibility, and all families helped each other. If a family arrived in Pecos with no money, our overseer would be sure to acquire the necessities for the family on credit or his word. When our paychecks came, he'd honorably cash them for us, pay our debts, and give us our money. We were not self-conscious about our economic condition. The only time we felt different was when we would go into little towns on our treks northward and not be allowed to enter a shop with five, six, and seven kids at a time. That used to hurt us because we knew we were not going to steal, but the owners had been burned before and that was that.

On the drive home after the final harvest, we children would bump along in the back of the truck watching the roads disappear behind us. The long return trips carried us by clusters of tiny, tidy houses in planned neighborhoods in towns like Lovington, New Mexico, or Seminole, Texas. I would feel pangs of hope and desire as the developments receded from view. The houses were modest and unadorned except for a couple of folding chairs or a flag in a socket, but they represented the security of the American dream. I loved my family. It was happy, healthy, robust, and loving, but I couldn't help hoping that one day one of these houses would be mine.

I often told my brothers and sisters, "Someday, if we study and work hard, we can all live in homes like this." Even at that young age, I knew what a great country we lived in and that these dreams were possible to fulfill.

Back in Redford, we settled in for the winter months. We shopped in Presidio for the school year, buying our one pair of new shoes, a couple of pairs of jeans, and some shirts. My mother purchased large sacks of beans, flour, lard, and potatoes to last us for a few months.

My mother, Esperanza, was a little woman, only four feet, eleven inches, but she packed a lot of determination and pride in her small frame. She gave our family great strength and was unwavering in her devotion for protecting us. We had very limited expendable resources, but she loved having her hair styled whenever she could afford it. When we were in Redford, she kept her thick, feminine fingernails manicured and her hands beautiful despite her hard labor in the fields. Her light skin took a beating in the sun, but she always kept a jar of Crema Esoterica in her bag to fade the sunspots. Her work ethic was so strong that she worked until she was past eighty years old, and if she had been allowed to do so, she would have worked longer.

My father, Salvador, usually stayed behind in Redford during our annual treks northward. He tended to the cotton crops that we planted on our own farm and took care of the small number of animals we raised. Truth be told, he probably could have worked harder and done better for us, but he was a loving man. He seemed larger than his five-feet, nine-inch frame, always standing tall and erect. His skin, like my mother's, was leathered and burned from the hot Texas sun. When my parents married, my father was twenty-five and my mother was fifteen. He spotted her in Presidio walking to school in her uniform and he fell in love. The courtship was short. My father promised that he would be good to her, and so with parental consent, they were married and took up residence in the smaller adobe house on the Acosta farm in Redford before starting their family.

My parents raised wonderful, loving children despite their scant resources. The official head count under our roof at any time was in constant flux, with older children moving out before younger ones were born. My oldest brother, Fernando, moved away when he was only thirteen to take landscaping work up north. This made me the oldest child at home, and I took my responsibility seriously.

That summer I got my first taste of gangs after a day of working the crops in Pecos, the pits of the earth. The King Hawks, a Hispanic gang, were influential in this town. They were extremely self-promoting, glamorizing their appearances with hard-core distinctive dress and slicked-back hair, and they brazenly popularized drugs, violence, and rebellious anti-authority behavior. They were locals, and we crossed paths with them when going to the movies on Saturdays and hanging out in town. They had possessions that any poor person would envy: nice clothes, jewelry, and an occasional low-rider car. They had attitude and I was tempted to join them.

One day Bobby Martinez, a fifteen-year-old initiated gang member, confronted me, looking for a fight. We agreed to settle our dispute behind my family's shack that evening. When I came outside with my younger brother, Leonard, and two friends, I was ambushed by their pack of thirty hoods, much older in age, brandishing chains. Needless to say, I lost the fight but won the battle. I was punched again and again, getting to my feet only to be just as quickly knocked to the ground. I didn't fight back, knowing my brother would be pulled into it if I did.

Each King Hawk self-tattooed himself with a cross and his mother's name. Counting on joining up with them, my cross was half finished before the fight. To this day I am stuck with this inky reminder of my near-miss initiation. However, I was never again lured into their world. This small brush with the King Hawks put me back on the right path. I was an important influence on my younger brothers and I dreaded the thought that they would get mixed up in gang life. In one moment I chose honest work and honor over a life of crime with lowlifes. The attractiveness of being a gang member went out the window when I saw that there was no honor with these individuals. I realized that they were nothing more than criminals.

When we returned home to Redford that fall, I concentrated on my academics. I also worked at a gas station in Presidio sixteen miles away to help my parents meet the bills. I had all the credits I needed to get my high school diploma at the age of fifteen. Upon graduation, I enrolled in college for a semester at the University of Texas at El Paso, but I was too young to feel I belonged.

With no opportunities for me in Redford, I headed to California, where I worked in a clothing manufacturing company in San Diego and in an airport restaurant in San Francisco. I returned to New Mexico to work on an oil rig. It offered great pay for grueling hours. One afternoon, when the crew was riding from our rig back to the central office in completely oil-soaked clothes, I saw sailors in service dress whites. They were coming out of a U.S. Navy recruiting station. Their dress whites alone sold me on the idea of joining the navy.

After some paperwork and a physical, I was soon in boot camp in Orlando, Florida. After training, I was assigned to Miramar Naval Air Station near San Diego, where I completed my first years of service. During the fourth and final year of my commitment, I volunteered for a tour of duty on the USS *Hancock*, an old World War II aircraft carrier. I loved being at sea and traveling the South Pacific, with ports of call in Hawaii, Japan, Hong Kong, and the Philippines. I felt proud to serve our country and represent our navy.

About the same time, an accidental encounter in my little brother's grade school changed my life. My mother had moved the family to Marfa, and I was there visiting them. She and my father had gotten divorced after thirty years of marriage. Marfa was seventy-five miles north of Redford, but had great services, stores, beauty shops, and even a train station. It was a beautiful crossroads town surrounded by open desert and mountains. Nothing much had happened in Marfa since the film *Giant,* starring Elizabeth Taylor, Rock Hudson, and James Dean, was made there back in 1956.

I was upset to learn that my little brother had been placed in a grade he had already completed. Because the family followed the crops, my mother had been late enrolling him. Although the mistake had been brought to the teacher's attention, nothing was being done. I was on my way to see the principal when out of the corner of my eye, walking down the stairs of the school building, I beheld the most beautiful girl I had ever seen. Technically, I had seen her before, as a second grader in Redford, playing in the schoolyard with her older sister, Rosario. Her adoptive father, A. M. Parsley, had been our school principal, and now they were here in Marfa, and she was a twelve-year-old eighth grader. I knew Terrie was in my destiny. I had to bide my time, but I had inherited determination from my mother and father. No matter how long it took, I knew that one day I would marry her.

Because of her young age, I couldn't reveal my feelings for her to anyone, so I sent postcards to her parents from my sea voyages, knowing she would see them. Then I'd ask my little brother, Leonard, who was dating her older sister, for updates. When I had satisfied my four-year naval commitment, I moved to Marfa to help my mom and enrolled at Sul Ross State University in nearby Alpine, majoring in business administration. I worked on my degree while remaining in the Naval Reserve. Most importantly, I wanted to be close to Terrie.

When she was fourteen, we danced for the first time at the wedding of my childhood friend Pablo Carrasco and his new bride, Nancy, in the aptly named town of Valentine, Texas. I gave her a silver ID bracelet and asked her to go steady. Fifteen months later Terrie and I were married in a beautiful ceremony in El Paso. I was twenty-two and she was two months shy of sixteen, but we had the blessing of her parents. We had both been raised in poverty and divorce, and we were committed to making our marriage and our futures different.

After the wedding, we rented a small one-bedroom apartment in a government housing project in Marfa. I didn't go back to school that semester. Instead I taught myself to drive big rigs and took a low-paying job hauling cattle through West Texas and southern New Mexico. Terrie often came with me, and we shared the open road. With my wife by my side, the work was more adventure than labor. I didn't want to be a truck driver for long. My intention had been to continue with a career in the U.S. Navy as an officer upon completion of my college degree. In the meantime, on a whim, I had put in an application with the U.S. Border Patrol. When I was called for an interview and offered a position, I accepted.

The U.S. Border Patrol was and still is a great and storied organization responsible for patrolling and securing our Mexican and Canadian borders. Until the reorganization of many federal agencies under the Department of Homeland Security in 2003, the Border Patrol was under the umbrella of the U.S. Immigration and Naturalization Service, the agency within the Department of Justice tasked with handling all immigration-related matters in our country.

Founded in 1924, the Border Patrol grew from 450 to 1,800 agents by 1976, which in reality was still inadequate, when considering the two-thousand-mile southern border of the United States alone, where most of the agents were assigned. Even with this small number of Border Patrol personnel, the agency reported arrests of one to two million immigrants attempting to enter the United States annually.

The sad reality was that many of those arrests were of the same individuals who had already been apprehended near the border, processed for removal, and taken back to the border and escorted back to Mexico. Instead of returning to their homes, they simply started their journey again.

Terrie joined me for a while during my almost sixteen weeks of training at the Border Patrol Academy in Los Fresnos, Texas, where I graduated fourth in my class of 112 trainees. I was stationed in Marfa for my one-year probationary training, proud to be back home in a position of distinction. The Marfa area was a very desolate part of Texas with not a lot of action.

During a portion of my first year, I was assigned to a team installing and repairing ground sensors along the border. The devices, placed along roads or paths used by immigrants walking northward, could tell a dispatcher and agents how many people were in a group and if they were following a certain path. This gave the ability to intercept them as they trekked northward through the large, remote area we had under surveillance. Besides tracking immigrants, we also checked eastbound trains when they pulled onto the siding in Valentine and stopped. We also manned temporary traffic check stations on roads leading from the border to Marfa and Alpine.

One Saturday, when I was alone checking sensors, I noticed a pickup truck parked near a little store in Candelaria, where smugglers often hung out waiting for Mexican immigrants on their way north. The driver seemed to be killing time, and I suspected he was waiting for clients. I parked behind some mesquite trees and radioed our sector headquarters dispatcher to advise him that a load was about to stage and requested a record check on the truck's license plate. The supervisor on duty instructed me not to take any action because I was a trainee and alone.

I continued with my surveillance and soon a man climbed into the bed of the pickup and immediately lay down out of sight. He was followed by eleven others who did exactly the same thing. The last one went inside the store and emerged with the driver, before they both climbed into the cab and drove away. My heart pounded, anticipating my first take-down.

Despite my instructions from headquarters, I tailed them, staying safely behind as the truck headed north toward Marfa, thirty-five miles away. An hour later, just a few miles south of the Marfa city limits, the driver spotted my vehicle, acceler-ated, and veered off the road, crashing through a wire fence and coming to a halt in a sand ditch two hundred yards ahead.

I screeched to the scene as the men dispersed in all direc-tions. Rock Henderson, an agent whom I had radioed, arrived to assist me. We soon captured eight men huddled near some brush. When we reported this to sector, our supervisor said we had captured enough people, but I refused to stop until we found the other four.

Back at sector headquarters, the illegal immigrants impli-cated the driver and the smuggler. They told us that they had been charged $250 apiece, were headed to Odessa, and had a contact driving them from there onward.

I called the acting prosecutions officer, since the decision lay with him whether to prosecute the smuggler or return the group to Mexico. Normally, groups were returned without prosecution, but the statements from these witnesses were compelling. The prosecutions officer decided to charge the smuggler with immigrant trafficking. I was extremely excited that my takedown was going to result in a criminal case. Border Patrol trainees, especially in a small station like Marfa, generally did not get a chance to work a case that went to prosecution. Although not a major arrest by any means, this investigation had given me my first taste of what I wanted to pursue in my law enforcement career. I was thrilled, but I realized that if I wanted to participate in more meaningful and sizable investigations, I would have to move to a different position and location, most likely at a completely different district office.

I had sincerely enjoyed my assignments here, checking farms and ranches for illegal workers, manning traffic check stations, searching trains in depots and sidings, and "watching the line," observing the border from parked vehicles. But I was ready to increase my responsibility. When a position as criminal investigator in the Chicago District Office was posted, I submitted my name for consideration.

The INS had more than thirty district offices throughout the country, including some in large interior cities. The district offices were responsible for overseeing inspections at land, sea, and air ports of entry; handling the administrative work in deportation cases and hearings; detaining and removing immigrants; running detention centers; adjudicating applications for immigration benefits; and finally, investigating and apprehending immigrants working unlawfully in the United States or involved in other types of criminal activity.

Each district had criminal investigator positions, attractive for agents in the Border Patrol because the job was two grades higher, agents worked in plain clothes, and the positions were in interior cities, where there generally wasn't a Border Patrol presence. District offices benefited from selecting Border Patrol agents because they had significant law enforcement experience gained through their service on the southwest border and had completed a rigorous course of training at the U.S. Border Patrol Academy, which included learning Spanish. I was excited when I learned the Chicago District Office had selected me to be a criminal investigator.

Chicago, My Kind of Town

CHICAGO SEEMED LIKE an unlikely place from which to handle U.S. immigration issues. However, our agency had started focusing on Chicago and U.S. cities that had become gateways for illegal immigrants hoping for employment. The immigrants thought illegal, gainful work away from the border would attract less attention from enforcement. When I arrived, the Hispanic population in Chicago was exploding, in part because of our immigration policy change in the mid-1960s that ended the Braceros program. During its twenty years from 1944 to 1964, the program seemed to satisfy two problems: the American labor shortage during harvest and the workforce surplus in Mexico. However, a surge in complaints about migrant abuse and legalized slavery caused our government to reconsider, and the Bracero program was terminated on December 31, 1964.

Huge numbers of braceros, dependent on the money they earned in the United States, chose to stay illegally instead of return to Mexico in the off-season as they had in the past. Many Mexicans moved away from the border to Chicago, where they sought jobs outside the agricultural sector. Friends and family soon followed. Opportunistic, callous human smugglers exploited the situation and the situation had grown out of control. Our agency's focus was now to address both the illegal residents and the smugglers who transported and abused them.

The Windy City was a far cry from the West Texas surroundings where my wife and I had spent our childhoods. I was now twenty-three and Terrie was seventeen. We had a five-month-old son, Gabriel. We weren't accustomed to skyscrapers, snowstorms, and the excitement of Chicago. I knew my decision was good for my career, but saying goodbye to my parents and siblings was difficult. These were the days of letter writing and calling long distance on special occasions only.

Still, Terrie and I were enthusiastic to be on our own. We spent the first couple of months getting adjusted to big-city life. Of course, our brand-new Oldsmobile Cutlass Supreme, parked outside our small studio apartment, was stolen within days of our arrival, along with the belongings we still hadn't unpacked from the trunk. The insurance company took ten months to settle our claim, leaving us without a vehicle. The blessing was that I did not have to pay for parking in our building, and I got to know the city by taking public transportation.

I was one of twenty-eight new trainees arriving in Chicago that October. We had between fifty and sixty criminal investigators to cover four midwestern states: Illinois, Indiana, Wisconsin, and Iowa. The functions of the district office were divided between four units: General Investigations, which handled issues related to immigration and fraud, such as a falsified marriage or a counterfeiting vendor; Special Investigations, which oversaw subversive and criminal inquiries related to immigration; Anti-Smuggling, woefully understaffed with only one agent assigned to our Chicago office; and Area Control, which was basically work-site enforcement, with agents in the field picking up immigrants where they were illegally employed.

The new recruits were assigned to the Area Control Unit. We visited various work sites known to hire immigrants, mostly restaurants and small factories, and identified the illegal workers. Although the job wasn't that glamorous, I invested myself fully in the work.

The sites were not chosen haphazardly. Every day, our office received reports from the general public, law enforcement authorities, and anonymous tipsters from workplaces that employed illegal immigrants. Generally, the tipsters were employees at risk of being fired or competitors hoping to cause trouble for their rivals. These reports listed the businesses, sometimes information on who owned them, and the names of immigrants employed, if known. Using this information, we organized the raids, some bigger than others, and made surprise visits. Many of these businesses had already been hit before. We would place agents near the rear exits to prevent workers from running, and a small team would enter through the front entrance. Permission was asked and generally granted from the managers or the proprietors to search the premises. Once inside, we questioned the employees and, if we found them to be in the country illegally, we took them into custody. For the most part, we had a good idea how many we were going to find at any location, as we oftentimes did surveillance for a couple of days and would plan accordingly.

When the inspection was completed, we offered those in custody the opportunity to visit their homes to pick up their belongings. Most of them declined the offer, not wanting us to know where they lived or to arrest other people who might be there. We took great pains to make sure that no children were left alone at their residences without a parent. Sometimes those arrested wouldn't divulge this type of information but we allowed them to call someone to see after their families.

Once our detainees were transported to the main downtown office, we filled out a "Form I-213, Record of a Deportable Immigrant" and if the individual wanted to fight removal from the country, we would issue an "Order to Show Cause," a bond condition whereby the immigrant would set up a deportation hearing. If he chose to go before an immigration judge, he would have to stay in custody until the hearing or post bond. The great majority preferred to voluntarily leave the country, because transportation was at the government's expense. They were boarded on buses within a day or two, headed for Mexico. Non-Mexicans from other Central American countries passed themselves off as Mexicans, thinking they'd have less distance to travel to make their way back.

If we encountered someone with a criminal record, he would automatically be set up for a deportation hearing with an immigration judge, which ensured that if he returned again, he could be charged criminally. The whole procedure was ineffective and a wasteful use of resources, as far as I could tell. Most of the immigrants counted on being back in Chicago within a few days, after a quick ride to the border and a fast negotiation with a familiar smuggler on the Mexican side. To them, deportation was only an inconvenience.

There is a huge difference in the way enforcement actions are handled by agents today. In my opinion, it's worse. A good example is the U.S. Immigration and Customs Enforcement (ICE) raid at the Agriprocessors meatpacking plant in Postville, Iowa, in May 2008. According to agents who worked on the operation, the raid had been in the planning for one year, utilized close to one thousand agents and other personnel, and cost more than $10 million to execute. Hosam Amara, a manager at the facility, fled to Israel following the raid but was ultimately arrested by Israeli authorities on April 11, 2011, and was awaiting extradition to the United States to face criminal charges. I applaud the action taken by ICE against the owners of Agriprocessors, who certainly deserved to be sent to jail, but $10 million to arrest 391 immigrants, fifty of whom were subsequently released?

When I was in Chicago, we only had a small number of criminal investigators assigned to our bureau, but given our resources our enforcement actions were very effective and we could handle the large numbers of immigrants we arrested.

Soon after my arrival in Chicago, I met Gary Renick. Gary asked me to participate in a sweep at O'Hare International Airport, an untested kind of interception at the time. A foiled stowaway attempt that had netted sixty illegal immigrants, almost by accident, had turned our focus to airports as a lucrative target. A Chicago-bound stowaway had managed to get on board an American Airlines flight from Los Angeles without a ticket. When he was discovered during a head count, the airline notified Chicago police, and officers were waiting for the plane. The stowaway was escorted off first.

"Follow me," a police sergeant directed. To his surprise, sixty other undocumented passengers also fell in behind him, thinking his command was for all of them. They were traveling together, assisted by unassociated smugglers in what was termed a "loose confederation," an arrangement where smugglers shared their resources, transportation arrangements, and guides.

When we decided to focus on O'Hare, we were hoping to snag the bigger fish: the smugglers and transporters. We knew the flights they used were typically red-eyes from Los Angeles because INS agents were not on duty and they were relatively less expensive. Before the 9/11 terrorist attacks, identification was not needed to board a plane, and tickets didn't have to be purchased by the flying passenger. American Airlines was the preferred carrier because they had numerous direct flights from the West Coast to Chicago.

Our team of four—Gary, me, Mark Cangemi, and the district's only other Hispanic investigator—arrived at the airport at four-thirty that first morning. We stood near the plane door looking for suspicious behavior, such as a passenger who followed someone without talking, avoided eye contact, or didn't answer to a "good morning" greeting.

We checked three flights over four hours, pulling fifty immigrants from the passengers. They were mostly men traveling alone, destined for Chicago to join family members waiting for them. They generally showed no reaction or emotion when we pulled them from the crowd exiting the gate, and submissively accepted that their luck had run out. Separating the smugglers from the *pollos* was impossible. No one was willing to say he was a smuggler, and nothing physical differentiated one group from the other.

Our team had secured the fifty we had taken into custody with uniformed immigration agents in the international arrivals building and was heading back to the domestic terminal when we encountered a group of Mexicans congregated around a bank of telephones. They had gotten off a flight we hadn't checked while we were preoccupied at international arrivals. One of the men was arguing in Spanish with someone on the phone, demanding money for smuggling fees. Gary and I understood every word and approached the group with our credentials in hand. I walked up to the ringleader and started questioning him, while Gary and Mark ascertained that the other individuals with him were in the country illegally. After a scuffle, we finally managed to capture our only verifiable smuggler in our four hours of work.

The O'Hare stings continued with mixed success. The number of captures started to dwindle when the smuggling operators in Los Angeles got wise to our program and changed their game. Over the next few years, we retired the program altogether because of complaints that we were profiling passengers. More importantly, offices located near the southwest border, such as the one in Los Angeles, stepped up their vigilance at airports to the point that they now have units assigned to those locations.

Commercial jets, trains, tractor trailers, moving vans, and private vehicles all delivered dozens of immigrants at a time, leaving them with relatives or employers in Chicago. Many smugglers were part of small family-run operations. More sophisticated family groups, like the Medinas, evolved into syndicates that controlled entire human smuggling networks.

Our system to keep track of the smuggling families and syndicates was not very efficient. U.S. Border Patrol antismuggling units did not share intelligence with the antismuggling units of the satellite offices in the interior, such as Chicago, unless it was done through personal relationships between agents. Each office had its own set of files and there was no cross-referencing of the information.

The INS was an immigration enforcement agency only. Securing the border against terrorism or threats to our national interest were always concerns but were not given the priority and attention that they deserved or that is given now. Because I was one of only two Mexican-American investigators in the Chicago District Office, I worked with General Investigations, Anti-Smuggling, and Area Control. The only unit I didn't work with was Special Investigations, with its ponderous amounts of legal work. I moved in and out of the other three as needed. My reputation for intelligence gathering and undercover excellence gave me great freedom to choose where I worked and which cases I wanted to pursue.

For the most part, I had the support and respect of my fellow agents, many of whom remain friends. A few may have resented that I was allowed to pursue major criminal investigations so early in my career. My optimism and enthusiasm remained strong in the face of such a daunting task—addressing, checking, and ultimately reversing Chicago's rampantly expanding illegal immigrant population. I was not deterred by those few complainers and worked my assignments with 100 percent heart and gusto, hoping that I could make a difference.

Despite being small in terms of number of employees, the agency had a lot of pride. Nationwide, we had less than eight hundred criminal investigators, fewer than the number of FBI agents in New York City alone. Yet we easily surpassed the arrests they made by the thousands. We encountered FBI agents who were surprised at how many arrests we handled each day and we were shocked that some of them had never made any.

We were often called in to cooperate with the FBI and other federal agencies because of the latitude afforded when enforcing immigration laws. For example, if an illegal immigrant was involved in a criminal activity such as smuggling or narcotics, we were able to take him into custody even if the criminal case had not yet been made. Many of the immigrants we detained were anxious to find a way to exempt themselves from deportation in exchange for inside tips and information on other criminal violators. Other agencies, such as the Drug Enforcement Administration, Bureau of Alcohol, Tobacco & Firearms, and the Social Security Administration, were always asking us to provide them with willing informants to help their investigations.

Our Chicago office addressed Chicago issues though, and for the most part, found it easier to apprehend illegal residents or workers and send them back across the border rather than expend our limited resources on extended investigations, such as the case that was active in El Paso against the Medinas.

In Chicago, it was mostly low-level drivers and underling

smugglers who were being convicted. These criminals were not considered high priorities by the U.S. attorney's office or the federal courts. Many times federal prosecutors would turn down prosecution requests because of the minimal penalties declared by the courts. The vicious cycle of capture, arrest, prosecution, and release was extremely frustrating to agents who were committed to making a meaningful contribution to the fight against immigration violators.

A few of us more inventive, courageous agents started brainstorming riskier operations usually involving someone operating undercover, to try to get to a previously untouchable crime boss. Because I was young and eager, and I partnered with dedicated, knowledgeable veterans, our investigative teams had a winning, confident attitude that served us well.

Counterfeiting was another one of the agency's targeted crimes. Fake birth certificates, Social Security cards, draft cards, and green cards were being sold to illegal immigrants, allowing them to establish identities, obtain employment, and, in some cases, avoid deportation. We wanted to infiltrate these operations, and when the opportunity arose to team with Roland Chasse, a reputable, veteran criminal investigator in Chicago, on the case of a legendary counterfeiter, Newton Van Drunen, I was delighted.

Newton Van Drunen was a forty-eight-year-old naturalized American citizen, born in Canada and raised in south Chicago. He had majored in theology and briefly ministered at the Mexican Baptist Church in South Holland, Illinois, before having his ordination revoked because of accusations of womanizing. He appeared to make monthly trips to Mexico, returning with illegal immigrants whom he provided with housing and fake social security cards for a fee. By his own admission to an Illinois state commission, he bragged that he had aided fifteen thousand illegal immigrants in one way or another.

In May 1970, he was stopped in Dallas for a minor traffic violation and had five illegal Mexican immigrants in his car. He was not prosecuted, the five immigrants were returned to Mexico, and they reunited in Dallas a day later. In January 1971, a Mexican laborer was found dead at a house rented by Van Drunen in Matamoros. This time Van Drunen faced charges of fraud, homicide, and immigration violations, but a shady judge dismissed all the counts against him. In August 1971, two Mexicans found in the trunk of his car in Encinal, Texas, also did not warrant an arrest or prosecution.

Van Drunen had many mistresses, some in Mexico and some smuggled from Mexico to Chicago. After one of them, Sara Resendez, had been detained, she willingly testified against her paramour in exchange for being allowed to stay in the country as a witness, and he was subsequently charged with human smuggling. He was convicted and sentenced to two years in Sandstone Federal Penitentiary in Minnesota. Agents knew he ran a counterfeiting operation, but they had never been able to get near it.

Prior to serving his prison term, Van Drunen had moved a large amount of counterfeiting equipment to the apartment of Oralia Ruiz, another of his mistresses. While he was in prison, agents used a contact to purchase Texas birth registration cards and birth certificates, and Selective Service cards from Oralia. The criminal investigators then raided her apartment and seized rubber stamps, plates for the production of immigrant registration cards, and hundreds of counterfeit documents. They also arrested Oralia, who provided a statement that her common-law husband, as she referred to Newton Van Drunen, had been directing the sale of the counterfeit documents from inside the Minnesota prison, where he had been assigned to work in the print shop!

Van Drunen was released from prison in May 1976 but never faced additional charges of counterfeiting despite overwhelming evidence against him. The information gathered by agents was ruled "hearsay," and witnesses were unwilling to testify against him in court.

Remarkably, Van Drunen approached several printing supply companies and purchased the materials he needed to restart his fake document business. He was back up and operating within a couple of months. He had a loyal lieutenant, Joaquin Alvarez, who was often heard boasting about the flourishing business while he was selling some of these documents on the south side of Chicago. Though he had been accused of killing at least one person in Mexico, police had not been able to make a case against Van Drunen. With his background and reputation, it was easy for him to maintain strict control over the distributors of his forgeries with threats of violent retribution, preventing his counterfeiting ring from being penetrated. Agent Roland Chasse and I hoped to get inside the operation by way of an unsuspecting Alvarez.

Successful counterfeiting stings were hugely dependent on informers and confidential sources from the counterfeiter's end of the business. Most of our tipsters were afraid to work against Van Drunen because of his power. My informant, whom I will call Francisco because of numerous threats on his life, was an exception. He was not only a gutsy, savvy, smart individual, but he was so reliable I used him in smuggling cases as well. Informers such as Francisco did a lot of the initial legwork on a case to minimize the exposure of the undercover agents.

During the briefing, Roland told me that Francisco had gained Alvarez's confidence. Francisco and other agency informants had already purchased counterfeit documents from him. Roland was confident that we could edge in on Van Drunen through him. Francisco was going to introduce me to this steadfast deputy later that evening.

Following the debriefing, I went home to change into clothes that would make me look more like a Mexican laborer. I was too naïve to understand the danger of undercover work and focused on the thrill as I explained the operation to Terrie.

In the early evening, Roland dropped me at Francisco's address and took up a position outside to keep an eye out for Alvarez. Meanwhile, I was basking in my good fortune of not only working the Van Drunen case, but also having a contact on the inside who was a superb cook. Francisco had prepared a huge pot of perfectly spiced chili con carne to entice Alvarez to join us for dinner when he arrived. Well past ten o'clock, we were interrupted by a loud knock on the door. Alvarez strolled in, crowing that his large number of document deliveries had delayed him. He didn't seem to feel a need to be discreet in front of me. Francisco introduced me, explaining that I was interested in purchasing documents.

As Alvarez spooned in mouthfuls of chili, I told him I had a list of people needing fake documents and immediately gave him the biographical information for my first "client." He spoke almost as fast as he ate, exalting his boss and abbreviating the long name to "Newt." I took advantage of the opportunity provided by his braggadocio.

"Perhaps you can introduce me to 'Newt,' and I can work directly with him? I need a quick turnaround on these documents," I said. Alvarez sat upright in his chair and spoke sternly. "My boss has no interest in meeting anyone else. If you want to purchase documents from us, it will be through me. Do I make myself clear?"

I suggested to him that he give me his own address and phone number, so we wouldn't have to keep meeting at Francisco's. Sensing that he was back in control, he wrote the information on a piece of paper and handed it to me. He promised delivery of my client's documents in two days and said the "old man," as he occasionally called Van Drunen, was always perfecting the quality of his works, including fake green cards, and I would not be disappointed. We'd meet again when they were ready.

Two days later, Alvarez called Francisco to let him know my documents were on hand and that I should meet him at Francisco's house. After I paid for the materials, I again boldly pressured him for an introduction to Van Drunen, promising him I would not cut him out on the profits. He was always very protective of his boss, but trusted Francisco enough to kill any suspicions that I might be an undercover agent. "Why don't you come to my house this Sunday?" Alvarez asked. "Newt will be there and we can talk to him together."

Early that Sunday, I went to Alvarez's neighborhood on

Chicago's south side, where most of the buildings were three-story houses rented by Latino families that had arrived during the recent immigrant surge. The neighborhood was relatively safe and quiet. Alvarez's house was easy to find, and I found him barbecuing in the little yard, despite the snow on the ground. When Van Drunen failed to arrive, Alvarez asked me to accompany him on a few deliveries and by the time we returned, Van Drunen had come and gone. The "old man" had been conducting his own surveillance of Alvarez's house, making sure no one had accompanied me. We were relieved he had not spotted Roland sitting across the street watching my back from a red Cadillac. But then again, this is what I would come to expect from Roland, a great and patient partner who in later years would come through for me during a cocaine bust that almost went sour.

Again I pressured Alvarez for an introduction to Newt, letting him know that expediency, not money, was the issue. I had twenty orders that I needed fast, and taking my order to the boss man directly would better serve us both. I would still pay him his cut.

"I can't introduce you. I'm too afraid of him," Alvarez responded. He handed me a folded paper. "Here's his address. If you want to work directly with him, do it yourself and don't tell him I sent you."

One day later, I was at Van Drunen's door, having walked there from the block where Roland had dropped me off. Now Roland was positioned across the street in his car.

"¿*Que quieres?*" Van Drunen asked in perfect Spanish when he opened the door. He was a huge man, large and dauntingly tall. His hairline was receding, appropriate for a man of his forty-eight years. His wire-rimmed glasses, slacks, and neatly pressed collared shirt made him appear more like a businessman than the unscrupulous boss of a major counterfeiting ring.

"Señor Van Drunen, I hear you are the best counterfeiter in the business. My name is Leonardo, and I am the best vendor on the streets and I want to work with you," I said, answering his question. I chose Leonardo because it was my brother's name. I was dressed like many of the young Mexicans in the neighborhood, worn work clothes, old shoes, and an inexpensive jacket from a thrift shop, too big by only one size. Without uttering another word, Van Drunen grunted and walked back inside, leaving the door open.

I waited a bit, then interpreted the open door as an invitation and walked straight into the kitchen, leaving my revolver holstered on my lower back. Van Drunen was seated at a small table; a woman who was either his wife or mistress was standing dutifully by his side.

Using a deep, intimidating voice, he growled, "I don't know who the hell you are. You're either a snitch for immigration or an FBI agent. Those clowns are always sending people like you over to my house."

I stared back at him. "I swear by my mother who is still alive, I am neither one of those two," I said, and made the sign of the cross. "I heard you were a great counterfeiter and a great boss to work for. I am here to offer my services."

"Who told you about me and who gave you my address?" he asked, slightly softened by my holy proclamation.

"Joaquin Alvarez gave me your name and address," I replied, showing him a small piece of paper Alvarez had written his name on. I knew he would recognize Alvarez's handwriting.

"I have told that son of a bitch never to do that," he replied. "But I will deal with him later. Sit down and we shall see if you really are who you claim to be. It will be easy to find out." He brought a bottle of whiskey and two glasses to the table and poured a shot in each glass.

After three rounds of whiskey and continuous pointed questions, he seemed satisfied with my well-rehearsed answers. He bought my story that I was employed at National Steel, a large company in south Chicago, and that I lived at 1232 North Bosworth Avenue with several other Mexican immigrants.

Like most crooks, Van Drunen bragged about how he had built up a defense around himself after having spent time in jail, and he had no intentions of getting caught again. He told me with a loud guffaw that the INS didn't have anyone intelligent enough to catch him. Several times he made a point of repeating the threat of the "severe penalties" he would impose on any of his associates who dared cross him. I knew he was letting me know the conditions of our relationship if, in fact, we started working together.

Finally, at eleven o'clock I gave Van Drunen a piece of paper with my alias and fake address.

"I will check it out, Leonardo," he said. "You just won't know when I'll show up. It might be one day from now or it might be a week. It might be in the morning, or it could be at midnight. If you really live there, I will find you."

"I will be waiting," I replied, relieved when he didn't accompany me to the car. "*Gracias, señor. Buenas noches, señora,*" I said to them, then retreated into the cold February night.

After confirming no one was watching me, Roland picked me up around the corner. We were both thrilled with my covert performance. The gravity of undercover work was hitting home—there were no "cuts," no "take twos," one chance only to be convincing to a shrewd, hard-marking audience. The role-playing part of it seemed to come naturally to me. As long as I was strong, aggressive, and even crass, I managed to make my targets switch gears—from initially being suspicious, to trusting and believing me. I knew when to back off and when to be charming. I also seemed to have a good gut sense for when things were unraveling.

Roland and I drove several miles to an all-night diner to take notes, discuss what events had transpired, and consider how the operation would progress. Roland prided himself in the meticulous observations he gathered as soon as possible, so as to remember important facts that would be needed later for search and arrest warrants. I gave him all the details, from the appearance of Van Drunen's wife to the undertones of his questions. Next we had to plan how I was going to be Leonardo, who was an employee at National Steel and a resident of 1232 North Bosworth. Roland had a contact with National Steel who would be able to list me on the books as an employee. I had a contact, Salvador, who lived at 1232 North Bosworth.

I had encountered Salvador, a young Mexican, during one of my early raids in Chicago when we inspected a south side restaurant. We had arrested sixteen Mexican immigrants who worked there, but Salvador seemed to have the required work visa. He lived with the others, which I thought was suspicious, a legal resident residing with so many immigrants in a very small house. Four of us inspected his document, but the fake was completely convincing, even up against our scrutiny.

I decided to test Salvador with a bluff. "I am going to take you in," I said. "If your document is good and the picture is the same as the one in the file, I will personally bring you back. If it isn't, you are looking at one or two years behind bars."

Salvador was a likable short, swarthy young man with an infectious smile behind his thick mustache. His expression changed with my question. After a hesitation, he asked, "If I tell the truth can you help me?"

Driving back to the office, Salvador and I started bantering and discussing immigration issues, employers who had large immigrant work forces, smugglers and their MOs, faked documents and their availability. I knew I wanted Salvador on our team. Gary and I went to our supervisor to ask if we could use Salvador as a contact and give him a permit to remain and work in the country. He soon became one of our best contacts in Chicago and would help us in a great number of major cases.

Salvador now lived with four Mexican immigrants on the north side of Chicago in a basement apartment at 1232 North Bosworth. I hoped he would be able to convince them to let me stay there for the duration of the investigation, probably a few weeks. I also needed to tell Terrie about my new living arrangements, but when I got home well past 2 A.M., I decided I would break the news to her in the morning. Gabriel was a great baby, but Terrie was so young that leaving them all alone in a strange city made me feel like I was shirking my responsibility. We always supported each other, and I knew she'd be okay with it. I'd check in as often as I could, but undercover missions were always risky.

The next day Roland called up his contact with National Steel and within two hours I was listed on the firm's payroll as a janitor. National Steel employed hundreds of people working multiple shifts, and we doubted anyone would seek me out personally. By 10 A.M. I had tracked down Salvador at the restaurant where he worked, and we discussed my plan. He was excited, already aware of Van Drunen. However, he may have spoken prematurely when he said his four roommates wouldn't mind me joining them in their cramped two-bedroom apartment. Soon after the midday rush, we went to North Bosworth. The neighborhood was a mixture of mostly Mexicans and Puerto Ricans, with a few Polish people left from past migration.

The crime rate in the neighborhood was high, with lots of reported muggings, burglaries, car thefts, and drug violence. However, the low rents and central location attracted many new immigrants. Buses and trains stopped nearby, making downtown easily accessible. The train stopped two blocks from Salvador's apartment. This was going to be an ideal location for me.

All of his roommates were home when Salvador and I walked in the door. The place was exceptionally clean. A small black-and-white television in a corner was broadcasting a program in English, and everyone was watching. Salvador told them I was moving in with them for a few weeks; he told them I was an old friend who had just arrived from California. The roommates were clearly not happy to have another person in their crowded quarters. After an animated discussion, they all left in a huff.

Salvador told me not to worry, things would settle, and

welcomed me to move in that night, February 8. "We just have to be careful they don't find out who you really are or they might tell the gringo," he said, referring to Van Drunen.

For two weeks I spent my time waiting for Van Drunen. My five roommates came and went with their daily routine, often having drinking friends and street hookers visit through the night for party sessions. Soon no one paid much attention to me. The days dragged on, and I barely went out, not wanting to miss Van Drunen.

On Friday evening, February 18, I took my first break from the cramped basement to spend time with Terrie and Gabriel. We watched a movie and relaxed in our small ninth-floor apartment overlooking Wrigley Field. I was overjoyed to be with them. I remembered when we were still living in Marfa, and Terrie had been thrilled to sign for a piece of mail with her married name. It was my acceptance letter from the Border Patrol, but signing for it as a married lady was what stuck in *her* mind. We still felt like newlyweds, but I had to leave early the next morning to go back to the North Bosworth apartment.

Salvador was pacing the small kitchen when I arrived, saying Van Drunen had come by at 1 A.M. asking for me. Salvador had answered all of Van Drunen's questions about me consistently, and Van Drunen had left satisfied. However, some of Salvador's roommates overheard parts of their conversation, arousing mistrust in me. Knowing Van Drunen's line of work, they assumed I must want to operate a counterfeit vending operation from their apartment. They were scared and upset. They had all paid coyotes to smuggle them into the United States, purchased counterfeit documents, and found jobs they wanted to keep. They were going to find out exactly what I was doing. I decided I would not leave the apartment again unless absolutely necessary.

A week later on a Saturday night, the apartment was filled with the typical ten friends and four prostitutes, as well as Salvador and his four roommates. Unbeknownst to me, in the mix of music, drinking, girls, and general chaos, Gustavo, one of my roommates, rummaged through my bag and discovered an INS criminal investigator ID. He didn't confront me, and I did not have any idea what he had done when I awoke that Sunday morning. I was the only one up when a knock on the door startled me. I opened the door to see Van Drunen standing there. He walked inside and I closed the door, pushed a chair his way, and started boiling water in a kettle on the stove. My five-shot Smith & Wesson was hidden in a never-used jar of instant coffee deep in the pantry by the stove. I hoped I wouldn't need to find it. I placed a couple of cups on the kitchen table by the window and closed the curtains.

"Are you going to sit down or do you want to drink your coffee standing up?" I asked. Van Drunen didn't take the chair and stayed on his feet near the door with his hands in his coat pocket, staring at me with suspicion through his thick glasses. When he finally spoke, he told me he wouldn't deal with me after all. I pretended to be indignant.

"You came all the way here this early in the morning just to tell me that?" I asked as I served him a cup of coffee and placed some breakfast cake on the table. "You could have saved yourself a trip by just forgetting about it." He seemed taken aback by my gall.

"I have told you," I said, "who I am, where I work, where I

live, and you still come asking questions about me. I told you I wanted to work with you and make some money for both of us. It's very simple. If you don't believe me, tell me. Either give me a chance or let's forget we met." I was gambling by being so impetuous, but I thought I had nothing to lose. He was on my turf now.

He finally lowered his huge frame into the chair.

"I am going to be direct with you again," Van Drunen said. "I have forty-three people that work for me, and I only trust five. I will give you a chance, but it will be a long time before I trust you. And remember what I told you when we first met. You cross me, you pay the price."

For a few moments we just sat and stared at each other. He was soon bragging about his operation. He told me he now had twenty different types of documents available, including birth certificates from two states, Illinois and Texas, Social Security cards, and union identity documents, and he wanted to know what type I preferred. I was back in business. I brought out the documents I had purchased from Joaquin Alvarez as if I needed more. In truth, I wanted him to say that he was the source of the fake documents so I could conclusively connect him to the conspiracy.

"I have better ones now," he laughed. "Let me know what you want. I will give you a good price, and you can triple your money when you sell them."

He set some rules. We would not use the phone to talk, and all orders would be picked up and delivered by him, but not at the same time of the day. Van Drunen explained that he liked to work at night to make following him more difficult. The previous night, he had delivered documents throughout the entire city. He seemed to like having a new audience to impress. I quickly placed an order for birth certificates for two fictitious immigrants, Ramon Anaya and Manuel Carrasco from Chihuahua, Mexico.

Van Drunen promised to have them delivered to me by the following Thursday. After he left, I sauntered into the living room. I hadn't been aware that two of my roommates were up, but when I joined them, they became suspiciously silent. I fumbled around the apartment, checking on my gun and credentials. Everything was in order, but I had a gut feeling something was wrong.

For a while I sat puzzled at the kitchen table. I was tired of being undercover, but I knew I had to keep it going. My favorite small comforts—unwinding with time by myself, reading the Sunday paper, or watching a game on TV with friends—were currently outside my reach. I missed my wife and baby, and I was feeling very unwelcome in the apartment, especially that morning.

The rest of the day was filled with uncomfortable encounters with Gustavo. I had no idea what his problem was, and I didn't care enough to ask. When evening fell, I left the apartment to get some fresh air. Gustavo rifled through my bag again, and took out my INS credentials to show to everyone. The others were stunned, with two even suggesting the ID was a counterfeit. They decided that harming me would lead to wrathful retaliation by the feds. But allowing me to pursue Van Drunen would result in worse retaliation from him when he was released from jail. They finally decided their best option was to tell Van Drunen who I really was, thereby earning his favor and getting rid of me without my knowing who had exposed me. Meanwhile, Salvador, who was supposed to be asleep, was listening through the bedroom door. A knock at the kitchen door brought all their discussions to a halt.

When Gustavo answered, he was met by the stare of Van Drunen. *"Necesito a Leonardo,"* said the old man. The roommates were speechless, but Salvador emerged from the bedroom. "What is it?" he asked. "Leonardo has gone out with a girlfriend and probably won't be back until tomorrow morning. He told me to take care of whatever you need if you came by."

Van Drunen eyed Salvador and the terrified roommates with great apprehension. Salvador ordered his four mates into the other room, making threatening eye contact with each one. Van Drunen was delivering the two documents I had ordered, although they weren't supposed to have been ready for a few days. "Give this envelope to Leonardo when he gets in," he ordered, handing Salvador the envelope. "He can pay me for them when I come again."

I returned three hours later to find the five roommates together, a couple of them visibly upset with their arms crossed, the television strangely turned off. I sat down slowly, looking each one of them in the eyes, and asked what was wrong.

Finally, Salvador spoke. He told me that everyone knew I was an undercover agent after Gustavo had found my credentials and showed them to everyone. He said his roommates had planned to expose me to Van Drunen, and he was trying to prevent that from happening. I was extremely disappointed in myself for being even slightly irresponsible with my ID. However, my being an agent might simplify things if I handled the matter strategically. I would have to negotiate carefully.

"Look," I said to the group, "now you know who I am. I need your help, but I can't really promise you much. If you tell Van Drunen who I am, I will make certain you are arrested. The agency already knows who you are. On the other hand, if you help me, I will talk to my boss and see if I can arrange to get you some permits to stay here legally as witnesses."

No one but Salvador said anything. "You cowardly bastards," he said to them. "It's time you all showed some balls. If we help Leonardo, we have a chance to get legal permits. If you guys choose to rat on him, I will personally take care of you."

The arguments always returned to a consuming fear of Van Drunen. Two mates mentioned going back to Mexico rather than getting on the wrong side of the "old man." When nothing was settled by midnight, we all went to bed. Salvador and I, shunned, had a bedroom to ourselves. I set up my bed to look like someone sleeping, fluffing up decoy pillows and covering them with my blanket. I spent the night sitting in a corner of the room, my gun ready at my side.

At six o'clock, everyone was up. I made coffee, but only Salvador wanted to join me. The others left the apartment without a word. "Don't worry," said Salvador. "They don't have the balls to say a thing. You can bet some of them won't even come back for a night or two."

That morning, I made a quick trip to district headquarters to discuss the situation with Roland. When I told him that my cover had been compromised, he volunteered to spend more time outside the apartment. We discussed twenty-four-hour surveillance with a team of agents but decided the risks outweighed the benefits. Those were the days when almost all the agents were conspicuously white.

Despite Gustavo's discovery and his agreement not to blow my cover, we were still pleased with the progress on the case. Van Drunen had delivered several Selective Service cards, some birth registration cards, and a number of Social Security cards, as well as a few other sample documents. We had all the evidence we needed to prosecute. Ted Giorgetti, the unit supervisor at the time, was part of the conversation. He knew Van Drunen personally from his smuggling arrest and was now in charge of making the decision to take him down.

Roland suggested we make one more undercover purchase from Van Drunen before we brought the operation to a close, and the higher-ups agreed. Roland and I strategized about the forthcoming week. When I arrived back at the apartment, I brought a case of Old Style beer to win my roommates over, if they were there. I was surprised to see them after Salvador said they might not be back. "I spoke to our director today and told him what happened here," I announced as I handed out the beers. "He wanted me to tell you how appreciative he was of the great sacrifice all of you are making to help me, and has assured me that you all will be treated right."

Gustavo was skeptical. "How can we know that as soon as you finish the case we will not be arrested?" he asked. "How can we trust you when you didn't even tell us who you were when you first came here?"

"Look, we can continue arguing here all night or we can enjoy our beer," I replied. "If something bad were going to happen to you, it would have happened already. I could've had you locked up so I could stay here in the apartment without having to worry about your bullshit until I finished the case. I chose not to do so. What is your decision?"

Gustavo seemed resigned to my remaining, and the rest of the group followed his lead. Salvador, too, was relieved. We drank our beers to songs from an album by Los Tigres del Norte, a popular Latino band. Ironically, one ballad glorified the exploits of a dope smuggler, Camelia la Tejana, who had an uncanny ability to evade immigration agents. Manny, the womanizer of the mates, went out and returned with his harem of Puerto Rican prostitutes, and the evening returned to its unconventional state of normal.

Even though I was more at ease with my roommates, the next four days seemed to drag as I waited for Van Drunen to return. Going to his place again would have been reckless even though I could have used the excuse that I owed him money. My roommates went to their jobs during the day, and I watched reruns of the Three Stooges. I looked forward to everybody getting back to enjoy the chili con carne I made in the afternoon. Twice I left the apartment at 2 A.M. to steal a couple of hours with Terrie and Gabriel, but I was always back by 4:30 A.M. My determination was firm, my confidence was charged, and my patience was steadfast. I'd wait out Van Drunen.

Finally, the Saturday night following the ID fiasco, when the typical party was in full swing, Van Drunen showed up. Seeing me in the midst of the celebration seemed to solidify my claim that I lived there. Although Van Drunen's arrival was not a welcome moment, my roommates continued their partying in the living room. The other guests were also unfazed by the big gringo in the kitchen.

Van Drunen seemed at home with a flock of illegal immigrants. Although I kept him isolated in the kitchen, he still assumed the posture of a Robin Hood of immigration, asking for a coffee with whiskey and contentedly taking a chair. He appeared to want to stay for a while, and I was happy to oblige him, hoping he'd start bragging. He did not disappoint me. Soon he was talking about the size of his operation and army of runners. I pressed for more.

"When do you have time to deliver to all these people?" I asked. "Why don't you let me work directly with you from your print shop and I can do your deliveries?"

"You will never be in my print shop!" he blurted. "I have forty-three distributors working for me, I only trust five, and you are not one of them." I had heard his lecture before, but he seemed to take pride in saying it again.

I poured him another cup of coffee with whiskey and snuffed out his interest in the ladies of the night in the living room by closing the kitchen door. Despite several drinks, he became annoyed by my prying questions and he abruptly got up to leave. Once again I scrambled to place an order with him to keep us connected. I asked for counterfeit documents for Reynaldo Valenzuela, a name I made up on the spot. I paid him for his previous delivery, which clearly softened him.

"I'll see you in a week or two," he said, rising from the chair. *"Buenas noches."*

From experience, I knew he would be back no later than a day or two. In fact, I was confident he would arrive Monday.

Roland and I met at the office very early Monday. He agreed with me that Van Drunen would show up at the apartment soon. By nine o'clock we met with Ted Giorgetti and the duty assistant at the U.S. attorney's office to let them know we planned to arrest Van Drunen the next time he showed up with the documents, which I predicted was imminent.

Roland and I decided we would both return to the apartment, and he would hide in the bedroom closet near the kitchen. I would once again try to pry information from Van Drunen about where his counterfeiting production was located. Since I had only spoken to Van Drunen in Spanish, the takedown signal to Roland would be when I said in English, "You are not going to believe this!"

Right before two o'clock that afternoon, we heard the knock on the door we had been waiting for. Roland ran into the small, dark bedroom. Just as Van Drunen had done when I went to his house, I opened the door, turned, and walked inside without saying a word. Van Drunen followed me to the kitchen table.

"Have a seat," I said. "Would you like some coffee?"

I boiled water for the coffee before he handed me one of the envelopes from his shirt pocket. Inside were the Social Security card, Selective Service card, and the birth registration card with the name I had given him two days earlier. I took a deep breath and exhaled deliberately. Van Drunen was ours.

Van Drunen gave me a curious look. I didn't realize my hands were shaking until I poured the boiling water into the two coffee cups.

"Tell me," I said. "Where do you keep all your printing equipment?" My question surprised him and he gave me a very awkward and suspicious look. He appeared to be trying to figure out who I really was. I didn't wait for his response. Grabbing my weapon from the coffee jar in the pantry, I said in a loud voice, "You are not going to believe this!"

Roland came out of the bedroom with his weapon drawn,

slightly unprepared because Van Drunen and my conversation had been so short.

"I am an immigration agent!" I told a stunned Van Drunen, waving my badge in one hand and my gun in the other.

I read him his rights. "Do you have anything to say?" I asked.

"Can I please have a glass of water?" he whimpered.

Van Drunen quickly regained his composure and asked for a lawyer. A search of his Chevy Suburban, parked in front of the building, was a jackpot of incriminating evidence. Inside the car Roland and I discovered a brown suitcase with thousands of counterfeit birth registration cards, Social Security cards, and Selective Service cards. We also found Texas notary public stamps, including one stamp in the name of Frank L. James; seals for Cook County, Illinois, and Travis County, Texas; paraphernalia for making stamps and seals; letterhead stationery from various companies; and printing machinery. We could only imagine what he had at his production facility.

After securing Van Drunen and the seized evidence, Roland and I escorted him to downtown Chicago for booking. Later that evening, agents from our office arrested Joaquin Alvarez as he arrived at his home. Roland and I stayed up late processing the evidence, and I didn't get home until almost ten o'clock. I arrived at the office early the next day, ready to proceed with Van Drunen's initial court appearance. I was the happiest I'd been since my wedding day as I walked into our office and the other agents heartily congratulated Roland and me on our case.

I was sure Van Drunen would be put away for at least five to ten years, especially given the fact he had a prior criminal conviction and had been in prison. Outrageously, the federal judge reduced Van Drunen's bond to $1,500. The asshole immediately posted it and left the courthouse, but not before sending a condescending, mocking grin my way. Of course, he didn't bother returning for his scheduled hearings, and a warrant was issued for his arrest.

Our federal judges, or the general public, for that matter, did not give that much importance to "victimless crimes," which many considered the selling of counterfeit documents to be. For criminals like Van Drunen and the thousands of illegal immigrants entering our country who needed the documents, the less attention given, the better. However, by not following through on opportunities to put these men away, we were doing a disservice to the hardworking, proud Americans who made an honest living. With counterfeit documents in hand, illegal immigrants could apply for health and education services without ever having to pay taxes. Even though this counterfeiter wasn't engaged in counterfeiting *money*, the money he cost the taxpayer was substantial.

Little information was received on Van Drunen after he was released, although sightings of him were sporadically reported to our office. I was absolutely certain Van Drunen was involved in counterfeiting again. He cherished the challenge of winning against the government, and he adored his reputation within the illegal immigrant community.

Four and a half years after he became a fugitive, we got our first solid leads that the gringo was back in business. A few weeks after our agency proudly announced the phasing in of a new counterfeit-proof "green card," costing several million dollars to develop.

Becoming a legal resident of the United States, or getting a green card, is the dream of millions of foreigners. Illegal immigrants can pay thousands of dollars to get the coveted card through fake marriages. Otherwise, fake green cards are the next best thing.

While our agency was doing its expensive revisions to get the foolproof cards to production, Van Drunen waited patiently. Within a few weeks of the press conference announcing the tamper-proof card, our informant Luis arrived at our office with perfect fake copies of the new cards. We set up a sting where Luis did business with distributors at a restaurant in West Chicago. Eventually we spotted our man, Van Drunen, in Joliet, Illinois, in a car as he was leaving a rented house that he used as a print shop. In dramatic fashion, we put him under arrest as he and his driver attempted to flee, dragging me with their car for almost one hundred feet. I was finally able to knock out the driver with my gun before the car crashed into a telephone pole.

"How are you, Mr. Van Drunen?" I asked my longtime adversary.

We had no idea what we would find at the Van Drunen house in Joliet. Against the back wall of the living room were stacks and stacks of blank vehicle titles, Social Security cards, union identity documents, Texas birth certificates, and birth registration cards, which are similar in size to a driver's license and can easily be carried in a wallet. In one of the bedrooms we found his printing press with more than three thousand counterfeit legal resident cards still on it. In the same room he had a desk with cutting equipment, chemicals, and material for his printing needs. Taking an inventory of the evidence took all night. The documents and printing equipment were of astoundingly good quality.

We spent the night logging the inventory. I was completely exhausted when I returned home the following morning. I had been on my feet for more than thirty hours. I shared the news of Van Drunen's arrest with Terrie and retired to the bedroom to rest. After sleeping for three hours, I found I couldn't move. Every effort sent waves of excruciating pain through my lower back. I remembered the scuffle during the previous day's arrest, which had sent me tumbling into the street. I'd sustained a considerable injury, but I hadn't realized it until now. At a local medical clinic I learned I had damaged my lower back badly enough that the doctor recommended I be hospitalized. I wheedled my way out of his office with the promise to stay off my feet, except for visits to physical therapy three times a week. The next day I was back at my desk.

Van Drunen would not fight the criminal charges we brought against him. He took full responsibility for his actions, which in federal crimes goes a long way to reducing a sentence, and he knew this. Following his arrest, Van Drunen testified before the U.S. Senate about his counterfeit document business, where he brazenly informed the committee that he had sold in excess of one hundred thousand documents in his career, although he refused to divulge the names or data of any of his subordinates or associates. Van Drunen was an innovator in marketing, distributing, and in controlling his illicit business. He saw the potential for a financial windfall with the ever-growing undocumented population in the United States.

The magnet that continues to draw illegal immigrants to the States, despite our best efforts on the border, is still the low risk to employers willing to hire an illegal workforce to keep wages low and profits huge. In an April 2006 raid of IFCO Systems Inc., a global pallet supply company, ICE agents arrested almost twelve hundred illegal immigrants and seven managers. The managers were described as systematically recruiting illegal immigrants, assisting them with transportation beyond the border, coaching them on how to avoid trouble with the police, and even helping them procure false identification. Master counterfeiters like Van Drunen thrive on this ready-made market.

The workers were allegedly given jobs in substandard conditions. According to Peter Smith, an agent in upstate New York, the ICE found workers "drilling, cutting, dismantling old pallets, pneumatic nail guns, power saws with most guys working in jeans, tennis shoes, short-sleeve shirts; some had sawdust in their hair."

Two years after that raid, I was asked to do an audit of two IFCO Systems sites in Indiana and Louisiana. Amazingly, I found that 40 to 50 percent of the workforce at the two locations consisted of illegal immigrants using counterfeit documents with stolen identities belonging to United States citizens. IFCO Systems reached an agreement with the U.S. government and agreed to pay a fine of over $20 million. Five of their top-level executives were criminally charged and were awaiting trial.

Amazingly, in September 2011, the senior executives of IFCO were allowed to plead guilty to only one misdemeanor count, despite the egregious actions listed in the Grand Jury indictment. Among them was an accusation that an illegal immigrant was using the Social Security number of a disabled American. The head of human resources at IFCO had been instructed not to verify that the immigrant was using the American's number. On another count, a defendant had forwarded an email asking what to do about a rehired employee using a "new and improved SS#" and whether they should "ignore and get him get two bogus W-2's for 2005." The response from the V.P. had been "I do not know what we have done with the W-2 on rehires, not sure I care. But let me know why I might care."

The pleas were surprising to both agents in the Immigration and Customs Enforcement and people in the business world who followed the case. The U.S. Attorney's Office in Houston never offered an explanation for why they were allowed to make their tearful pleas before a federal judge. Speculation is that despite the actions taken by these individuals, the government's ability to prove the charges was apparently at risk.

With this ready-made market, the sale of counterfeit documents has grown to be a multimillion-dollar business. Of even greater concern is the easy accessibility of counterfeit documents by individuals seeking to harm our communities and our country, as was the case with the 1993 World Trade Center bombing and the nineteen hijackers who attacked our country on September 11, 2001. Every one of these participants used multiple identities and counterfeit documents after they entered the United States with genuine visas issued by the Department of State.

"Fraudulent documents give people the appearance of lawful status and provide them a ticket to access and opportunities to which they are not entitled," ICE director John Morton stated in December 2010, in response to the indictment of twenty-two members of a sophisticated and violent counterfeit document ring.

CHAPTER FOUR

The Castillo Family

THE CASTILLO FAMILY was a force to be reckoned with. They were huge in the Los Angeles area, and so well organized that it was almost impossible to get inside them. The Castillos had been in business for years. We had no idea how the hell we were going to take them on, but I was confident we'd figure out a way to infiltrate their human smuggling ring. Their blatant disregard for our laws had to be challenged. I thought getting inside the pipeline would be the best way to handle it. I was not sure how it would play with my bosses, but I started drafting a plan.

The Castillos based their business in Los Angeles, but Chicago was their main depot. The *pollos* were crossed from Tijuana, Mexico, into San Ysidro, California, then hauled the

150 miles to Los Angeles. From there they were moved to Chicago for distribution to other points throughout the country.

With the help of informants, I learned that Domingo Perez, a legal permanent resident originally from Durango, Mexico, was one of the Castillo's main distributors in Chicago. As luck would have it, Francisco, our great confidential source from the Van Drunen case, knew Perez well enough to approach him.

Perez was soon using Francisco as a driver. He needed drivers to pick up new arrivals at the Joliet train station, forty miles from downtown Chicago, and deliver them throughout the metropolitan area. He was afraid to let the *pollos* wait around the station for long. They tended to stand out, not only because of their dress but also because of their habit of walking in a single file behind anyone who acted like a leader. They were so conspicuous, it amazed me that large groups made it as far as Chicago without being apprehended by our immigration authorities in Los Angeles or along the way. Yet I understood that it was impossible to detect and arrest the thousands that were crossing on a daily basis, given the limited number of agents assigned to protect our borders and even fewer resources dedicated to the interior INS offices. It would not be until years later, after the 9/11 attacks, that we were given the resources needed to address illegal immigration. By then millions of illegal immigrants had already settled comfortably throughout the country.

Perez began to trust Francisco enough to confide that the smuggling operation was headed by a husband-and-wife team living in Los Angeles. He described them as running a very tight organization, composed mostly of many family members and immigrants from their home state of Michoacán. Everyone knew each other, so infiltrating the organization was not going to be easy. However, Francisco was able to get the phone number of Agustin and Dona Carmen Valencia de Castillo in Los Angeles, and he passed it to me.

The two had settled in Los Angeles twenty-five years earlier, after Agustin immigrated from Mexico, and married Carmen, a U.S. citizen. Together they were one of the most formidable couples pursued by U.S. immigration authorities for immigrant smuggling.

The Castillos operated on a referral basis, only accepting clients who were friends or family members of clients who had already used their services. We entertained the idea of sending informants from Mexico to Chicago through the Castillos' pipeline, but the mission was too risky, so we ruled it out. We needed direct and convincing testimony from a trained agent, along with the required physical evidence, such as copies of wire transfers, ledgers with names and contact points of individuals who had been smuggled, and even recorded conversations, to dismantle a smuggling organization like this one and there was only one way to do that. I would go undercover using the family name of a recent arrival and have myself smuggled into the United States, then transported to Chicago, similar to my Juarez-to-Chicago assignment.

I called the telephone number Francisco had given me. A woman with a pleasant voice on the other end of the line told me she was Dona Carmen and asked what I needed. I thanked her for taking my call and informed her that I was phoning from Chicago and was interested in having my brother and uncle brought from Mexico. Dona Carmen asked me the name of the person who had referred me, then told me to hold the line. She was soon back on the phone telling me she had verified the name through her records.

With the referral confirmation out of the way, she quickly got to business. They had arrangements with several hotels in Tijuana. Even if my brother arrived without funds, all he had to do was tell the management at those hotels that he had been sent by the Castillo group, and he would be taken care of. She said the smuggling fee was to be paid upon delivery to the final destination.

Because of the Castillos' success, they were not afraid to deal with immigrants who didn't have the money to pay them in advance. Unlike other smuggling groups that formed loose, independent partnerships, with each faction operating a leg of the journey, the Castillos had a well-defined business structure from the originating location to the final distribution point. They also had an endless supply of business, knowing that their clients trusted them and referred all their friends and family. Clients also knew they would not be ripped off along the way. In delegating the fee collection duties to close and trusted family members in the Chicago area at the end of the line, the Castillos kept tight control of the financial part of their business.

During that first conversation, Dona Carmen recommended the now-defunct Alaska Hotel in Tijuana as one of the better places to stay. She assured me they treated her clients well, were trustworthy, and were protected by local cops on the take. This guaranteed that other cops would not try to rip them off and gangs would not prey on them. I said I would give the information to my supposed brother and uncle, Fernando and Arturo Ramirez. Dona Carmen politely told me she would be waiting for them, but she asked that someone in the hotel telephone her as soon as my relatives arrived in Tijuana. She promised me that my relatives would not have to be there more than one day.

After my conversation, I submitted a proposal to the INS regional office requesting permission to travel into Mexico and have myself smuggled through the Castillo pipeline. The U.S. attorney's office in Chicago wholeheartedly supported the plan. However, because of budget concerns, only one agent, me, was going to be able to go undercover. After my Juarez ordeal, I would have liked another agent with me, especially for backup, but I had enough faith in my abilities that I didn't hesitate in moving on.

With approval to go forward, Gary and I once again started planning my trek. I asked our Los Angeles office to check out the Castillo safe house at 6901 Compton Avenue. The agent from Los Angeles confused me when he said he couldn't find such an address. I knew the house existed, because I had been able to get telephone tolls of the number at that exact address. The agent had not gone out to check the residence, he had merely looked at a street map and when the street appeared to end at the 6700 block, he assumed the address I had provided did not exist.

When the confusion was behind us, I called Dona Carmen again to let her know my relatives were on their way to Tijuana. She reminded me about the Alaska Hotel and told me they had a backlog of clients in the pipeline, so I could expect some delays between Mexico and Los Angeles.

Although I didn't have another agent with me, I decided to bring one of our most reliable confidential informants, a man in his fifties named Arturo. He was someone we regularly used to infiltrate counterfeit document and immigrant smuggling rings. He had left a wife and six children in Mexico when he first came to the United States from Durango, almost seven hundred miles from the border. He grew interested in coming to the United States after learning of his brother's success in Chicago. Because he had a good job, a house, and a family in Durango, he qualified for a border crossing card, which allowed him to visit legally. Once here, he found a job that allowed him to use his construction and carpentry skills. Eventually he brought his family to Chicago.

He was always willing to help us and performed exceptionally well in undercover situations. In return we granted him work authorization and a permit to travel to Mexico once a year to visit his family. Without even asking what was involved in a mission, Arturo was always up for the challenge. I sensed that he liked the adventure as much as anything, was grateful to be in the country, and particularly enjoyed working undercover with me. On this mission, he even paid his own way to Tijuana.

As with most of my cases, I was very up front with Terrie. She was resigned to my determination to go after the major violators, regardless of how dangerous the mission. In fact, she knew I enjoyed the challenge of matching wits with these criminals. She was a loving and supportive partner whom I could count on to be waiting for my phone call if I needed help, just as she had proved to me during the Medina case. I often thought she enjoyed the chase as much as I did, but still, it never got easier. Even though I would have a trusted informant with me, the Castillo case made us both nervous.

My first stop after leaving Chicago was Los Angeles. I scouted out Compton Avenue, where the Castillo house was located. It looked like any other nice middle-class neighborhood. Their home on the corner stood out with its lush, neatly trimmed bushes and trees in a tidy green yard. An elderly man was watering the lawn in front of the house, which looked like it had recently been painted. Whoever lived there took great pride in it. Anyone passing through the area would never guess that thousands of illegal immigrants had passed through there over the years. I assumed a small, detached building in the backyard was the temporary housing for the immigrants.

The following day, I took off for the border accompanied by Rick Sanders, a criminal investigator in the San Diego office. Rick had once subdued a gunman, an armed immigrant intent on killing the district director in the Los Angeles office. Luckily, the shots already fired had missed their target before Rick jumped on the shooter from behind and dragged him down.

Our first stop was the Chula Vista Border Patrol Sector (now called San Diego Sector) to brief the chief patrol agent of our operation. I did not want a repeat of anything like the incident in New Mexico, when the state trooper had no idea who I was. I was expecting praise and strong encouragement for the mission, but I was wrong. Instead, the chief patrol agent informed me I would have a difficult time getting through their sector and my operation would probably fail. I felt like telling him that everybody else was sure making it through, but being respectful, I decided to let it go. Not easily discouraged, I thanked him and told him I would call him from Chicago when the investigation was completed. I left his office more committed than ever. That afternoon, I visited my eldest sister, Magdalena Hendrix, in National City, California.

My family has always played an important and encouraging role in my life. My sister and her husband, John, were surprised and happy to see me. As with everyone in my family, they were concerned about my safety when I was working undercover cases, especially ones in Mexico. John gave me his baseball cap from his Vietnam days for good luck. I resisted, knowing how much it meant to him, but accepted it when he wouldn't take no for an answer. The baseball cap turned out to be luckier than I could have imagined.

Rick dropped me off on the U.S. side of the border and I slowly made my way into Tijuana on foot, passing the hundreds of people lining up to walk or drive into our country. With my usual disguise, old faded jeans and shirt, I looked like most of the young Mexican men returning from a work assignment in the United States or being returned by immigration authorities. No one paid me any attention, with my little tricky bag holding a change of clothes and minor toiletries. This time, unlike the Medina case, where I had to seek out random smugglers in a Mexican bar, I already had my smuggler lined up and knew where I had to go.

The Alaska Hotel was not hard to find. Arturo, reliable as always, had already arrived following a short visit with his family in Durango. As far as Dona Carmen was concerned, I was Fernando Ramirez, the "brother" being smuggled, and Arturo was the "uncle." The hotel had seen better days, but it was far superior to El Correo in Juarez. A large group of people was gathered in the hotel office talking to what appeared to be a smuggler. Arturo had already gotten a room for us with two twin beds. As Carmen had instructed, I went to the reception desk to call her and tell her we had arrived in Tijuana. The conversation was brief. Dona Carmen told me to wait in my room and expect her workers to arrive in a few hours. She cautioned me not to give them any money, even if they demanded it. All payments were on the back end. Judging from what she said, we would be leaving that evening.

Several hours later, a loud knock on the door startled Arturo and me from our sleep. As soon as I unlocked it, two men shoved their way into the room, wanting to know how many of us there were and demanding money up front. I told them I had just spoken to Señora Castillo and she wanted to make sure I didn't pay any money up front. I told them we could go to the front desk and call her if they didn't believe me. Besides, I said, "Señora Castillo already spoke to my brother in the U.S. and he is going to pay when we get there." They realized they weren't intimidating me, and they backed off from their demands, telling us that that night's group was filled and we would not leave until the following evening.

Soon we heard them knocking on the doors down the hall, trying to get money from other clients. I was tempted to go down the hall and tell them to go to hell, but I used better judgment. From the noise, it seemed our smugglers had quite a number of clients at the hotel. These guys were open about their business, not worrying about any Mexican police.

Arturo and I decided to get a beer. Walking down the crowded Tijuana streets, we heard accordion music coming from one of the bars on the strip and decided to go in. The place was packed with smugglers and immigrants passing the time before continuing north. Several of the smugglers were outboasting each other about how much jail time they had served or how clever they had been at outwitting *la migra,* immigration officials.

All too soon it was one o'clock in the morning, much later than we had meant to stay. We slowly made our way back to the hotel, being careful not to get mugged on the crowded but dimly lit streets. We stopped at the front desk to pick up our key and were surprised that we had a message from the smugglers, telling us to be ready to leave at 4 A.M., three hours away. I went to find a pay phone to alert Rick Sanders about our departure time.

I had three hours to get some rest, or so I thought. I lay down on the small twin bed with my clothes on and fell into a deep sleep. I thought I was dreaming when I heard loud knocks on the door and someone yelling for us to get up. Arturo and I had only slept one hour before being awakened by the same two guys who had visited us earlier. As with many smugglers, these guys were known to the immigrants only by their nicknames. We got "El Chupon," which can mean pacifier or sucker, and "El Gringo" as our guides. Both men reeked of alcohol. Other smugglers in the hotel were picking up their clients at the same time, creating a bustling excitement and anticipation among the people getting ready to leave.

When we reached the parking lot, several minivans were waiting. El Chupon and El Gringo opened the back door of one and pushed Arturo and me in. The driver slowly drove around to the corner of Calle Primera to wait for other smuggling guides picking up their clients. We were soon joined by "El Ronco," "Murdullo," and "San Martin de Porras," and their clients, including two young girls about six and eight years old.

After driving for about two miles, our smugglers ordered us out of the minivan and told us to start walking. We walked an hour through brush and rugged terrain, at last coming to a steep hill, which overlooked a road that traveled to the U.S. side of the border. Our group totaled seventeen immigrants plus at least five smugglers. We were not the only ones waiting to cross. I saw similar groups hiding in the brush waiting for their transportation, too. I tried to take a mental count, but there were just too many of them. Suddenly, as if on cue, four men appeared and walked from one group to another demanding money. Mexican cops, not here to protect and serve, but to extort. I was really ticked off when one of the smugglers asked all of us to chip in before the cops reached us.

"You have to pay or they'll come back," he insisted.

I was relieved they were only crooked cops, not one of the criminal gangs that prey on the immigrants. They usually rob their victims of everything they have and often beat them. I had my old reliable wallet-size.25-caliber handgun in my rear pocket, but luckily no one searched me. I suspected the smugglers were in on the shakedown and I doubted these guys were even real police.

Each of us chipped in twenty dollars and they were on their way.

El Chupon pointed at several of us and barked, "You, you, and you will be riding in the trunk of the first car!" He instructed us to jump into the trunk as soon as the car arrived.

"No way I am going to ride in the trunk," I told him.

El Chupon just smiled. "Okay, then jump into the backseat on the driver's side." From a distance we saw two beaten-down cars approaching. "Those are our vehicles!" he yelled, pointing to a blue 1968 Chevy Nova and another small car. "Everybody run!" As the two cars started to slow, we scrambled down the hill. Several of the immigrants lost their footing and a few rolled down toward the bottom. If this hadn't been a serious moment, it would have seemed funny. It was complete chaos as everyone tried to get into the two small cars. El Chupon nimbly made it down the hill and was standing by one car, screaming for everyone to jump in. I ran between the two cars, reaching the right rear of the front vehicle. The next thing I knew, I was inside the trunk trying to regain my senses. I had a pain and ringing on the left side of my head. El Chupon had punched me and shoved me into the trunk. The claustrophobia I felt was overwhelming. I tried to straighten my legs, but without success, because there was someone on top of me. I managed to wriggle my way out. The body next to me remained frighteningly still as I pushed it to one side.

I asked myself, how could I have not seen this coming? We were traveling at a great speed. I knew we were riding overloaded because the rear of the car scraped the road whenever we hit a bump.

Just when I thought it couldn't get any worse, I smelled exhaust fumes that must have been coming in through a hole somewhere in the bottom of the trunk. "Are we going to die in here?" a scared voice asked, snapping me out of my panic.

"Not if I can help it," I replied. "I won't let this be our coffin. I will get us through this."

"If we suffocate, will somebody find us?" he asked, seeking some reassurance from me. He was sixteen and traveling alone to find his parents in the United States. His quivering voice startled me. I was a U.S. government agent on a mission and I felt responsible for him, as if he were in my custody. I felt around with my hands, looking for something to plug the hole that was letting the fumes from the exhaust pipe in. We didn't have much time before the carbon monoxide would suffocate us. As good fortune would have it, I was wearing the lucky cap my brother-in-law had given me. I knew the cap would work. I removed it and placed it over the hole, stopping the smoke. The lucky cap had done its part.

With the immediate danger over, my trunk mate started sharing his story with me. He said his name was Ramon. He had not seen his parents for almost five years, not since they had been smuggled into the United States. He had remained in his homeland, El Salvador, with two younger siblings and their elderly grandmother. He had been traveling alone for more than two weeks after getting separated from an older relative along the way. They had been sneaking around one of Mexico's many checkpoints when they lost each other.

Ramon didn't know if his relative had been arrested or killed, or was continuing on his own. Once he realized he was alone, he had sought protection from an older countryman with their group. But, after the pervert tried to molest him, he decided to run away. Somehow he had made it to the Alaska Hotel. The people at the front desk referred him to the Castillos. The Castillos telephoned his parents, who hired them to get the young man across the border.

Being locked in the trunk of a car was probably one of

the most exasperating situations I encountered during my undercover operations. I felt completely out of control and the claustrophobic feeling was killing me. I couldn't imagine what it must be like for Ramon. He had already seen so much horror. Thinking it would all end here in the trunk must have been unbearable. Here he thought the ride in the car across the border was his endgame to freedom. Instead the chances were great that this was his endgame to death. The children traveling across the border, many without their parents, were exposed to the same travel conditions as the adults; no "women and children first" in this world.

I did my very best every time I encountered these young, vulnerable children to shepherd them and protect them from the many uncaring bastards that smuggled them and didn't give a damn if they reunited with their families or not. It was my responsibility as an enforcement officer but on this count, I took it more personally. How anyone can treat children like this is beyond me. I would do my part to make sure these shitheads went to jail.

Ramon and I banged around together in the trunk, around curves and over bumps, often with tires screeching. After a while we seemed to have gotten to a better road because the ride became noticeably smoother.

I tried to imagine where we might be. My eyes had adjusted to the darkness by now, so I pried a small screwdriver I found in the trunk into the latch, while Ramon held my baseball cap over the hole. Surprisingly, the effort paid off. I popped the trunk but carefully kept the lid down so that the crack was only a couple of inches high. With the fresh air flowing in, I felt more optimistic and in control.

1968—Shack in Pecos, Texas, where we stayed when we traveled north to work in the fields. Sometimes eight of us stayed here at a time.

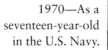

1970—As a seventeen-year-old in the U.S. Navy.

1972—With my mom on Mother's Day while on leave from the U.S. Navy.

1975—On our wedding
day in El Paso, Texas, on
September 13, 1975.

1976—Terrie and I at Border Patrol
Academy Graduation—Los Fresnos,
Texas. (Credit: Augustine Salacup)

1976—Border Patrol Academy
graduation.

1976—Marfa Border Patrol Sector—between Marfa and Valentine, Texas—with a group of illegals that Border Patrol Agent Jimmy Harris and I tracked for several hours. (Credit: Jimmy Harris)

1978—Medina Case—November 1978, after arriving in Chicago. We are in the basement parking lot of the federal building. I am in the middle and Gary Renick is on the right. I am still carrying my little "tricky" bag I took into Mexico.

1978—The Marquez Family: For their safety and to prevent abuse by smugglers, Consuelo Marquez (kneeling in front) kept her family close. Seven family members were smuggled by the Medinas to rejoin their father Pedro in Chicago.

1979—In Chicago following the seizure of hundreds of counterfeit legal resident cards, several handguns, and almost $15,000 in cash from a counterfeit document distributor on Chicago's South side.

1982—To my right is Special Agent Gilbert Wise on the day we took down Operation Villasana in El Paso, Texas. The I&NS Commissioner called it the agency's biggest smuggling case in a press conference. Gilbert and I did Operation Prieto together two years later. He died in a car accident after his retirement. (Credit: Dionisio Lopez)

1984—Houses where illegals were housed were called "wetshacks." I spent several days in this one at a tree farm north of Dallas where the owner kept about ten illegals cutting trees and allegedly refused to pay them their due wages. It was hard work, and I sure was glad when agents came in with a warrant. (Credit: Doug Keim)

1984—I am on the left, Tony Sifuentes is in the middle, and Special Agent Gilbert Wise is on the right during Operation Prieto. During this meeting, Sifuentes told us he could smell the "feds" a mile away. (Credit: Dionisio Lopez)

1989—I am on the upper left with Gilbert Rodriguez, Noe Dominguez, and Henry Aguilar after taking down a forty-five-pound cocaine case in Miami.

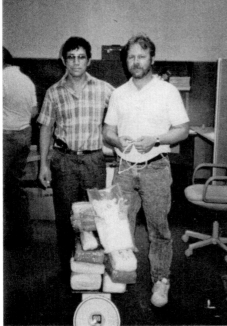

1989—With my brother-in-law, Harry Betz, following the undercover cocaine seizure in Miami. Harry would play a crucial part in a later case.

He produced three batches of phony money before the most recent one. He called them inferior, and said they had been "shipped" against his will.

The batch seized last week, he said, was intended to be another preliminary batch, to be followed by a fifth, "perfected" batch.

"None of this stuff was fit to go anywhere, because it wasn't finished," he said.

Van Drunen, a Canadian-born U.S. citizen, said he will fight "tooth and nail" any attempt by U.S. authorities to extradite him to the United States. He said he's already obtained an *amparo*, the Mexican legal document that protects its holder from prosecution in a foreign country.

Van Drunen, who talked for about an hour Friday afternoon with reporters from the Herald-Post, was surprisingly revealing about his career and his plan for counterfeiting.

When told about the interview, Driscoll warned against taking seriously all the claims made by Van Drunen, who also has been talkng to Mexican reporters.

Among Van Drunen's other contentions:

↗ Though earlier inferior shipments of phony money over nearly 2½ years totaled less than $1 million, he shipped $4.5 million of the most recent batch in the few weeks before he was arrested.

Driscoll, who interviewed Van Drunen at the time of his arrest but has not talked to him since, doubted that much had been shipped.

And he also doubted a recent report by Mexican authorities that recent large seizures of U.S. counterfeit money throughout Mexico could be linked to Van Drunen.

↗ Van Drunen also said — in reference to reports attributed to Mexican Attorney General Javier Coello Trejo that the accused counterfeiter may be linked to the Medellin, Colombia, cocaine cartel — that he knew of no such link.

↗ Van Drunen denied the attorney general's contention that he had passed about $100,000 worth of phony money to an El Paso Bank.

↗ This was Van Drunen's first venture in counterfeit money, though he has served more than two years of a 10-year federal prison sentence for counterfeiting U.S. immigration documents.

↗ He was planning to use capital he raised in the counterfeiting operation to develop a seawater desalination plant in the state of Tamaulipais, Mexico.

In connection with the latter claim, Van Drunen lamented that his contributions to society would be forgotten but his notoriety remembered.

And then he quoted Anthony's lines fom Shakespeare's "Julius Caesar":

"The evil that men do lives after them,

"the good is oft interred with their bones."

Counterfeiter blames pal for downfall

A boast of skill from Juarez jail

By Tom Tolan
El Paso Herald-Post

An accused counterfeiter Friday admitted producing millions of dollars in bogus currency and boasted of his craftsmanship.

And he blamed his arrest last week on a business partner he called an "idiot" and a principal customer he said betrayed him.

"Basically, I am an excellent technician," said Newton Van Drunen, 60, in an interview Friday at CeReSo city jail in Ciudad Juarez. "I don't think that there's any question left, anywhere in the world, about that."

But he went on to blame his business partner, an El Paso man, with pushing him to distribute the counterfeit bills before the printing process had been perfected.

Van Drunen was arrested in Zaragosa, near Juarez, a week ago by Chihuahua State Judicial Police. Officials say they seized $12.6 million in counterfeit money at the time of the arrest.

Bill Driscoll, agent in charge of the U.S. Secret Service's El Paso office, said the haul was one of the 10 largest amounts of counterfeit money ever seized.

Newton Van Drunen

Van Drunen did not deny being caught with the money, but he disputed government figures for the amount seized.

"I couldn't tell you the exact figure," Van Drunen said. "I figured it was $9 million. There was a large amount of stuff that was never intended to be used. It was experimental . . .

"We were testing papers, we were testing printing processes, we were testing a new ink."

Van Drunen said he had been perfecting his counterfeiting craft since he moved to Juarez in February 1986, after jumping parole in Illinois.

■ **SEE VAN DRUNEN**
/ BACK OF SECTION

1989—Newspaper article and picture of Newton Van Drunen following his arrest in Ciudad Juarez, Mexico, for possession of millions of dollars in counterfeit money.

1996—With Gladys Board and David Ramirez just before we arrested her at a lounge at the Holiday Inn in McAllen, Texas.

Pasaban Gente por Laredo

Atrapan Band

EAGLE PASS/VILLA DE

LOC

SECCION
C

EL PRONOSTICO PARA PIEDRAS NEGRAS

Sabado — Tormentas Aisladas. 31/21
Domingo — Tormentas Aisladas. 31/18
Lunes — Parcialmente soleado. 29/18

Ernesto Sandoval Peña (a) "El Zorro" (de izquierda a derecha), Enrique Flores Hernández y Juan Manuel De la Cruz.

Tres miembros de una bien organizada banda de falsificadores de documentos y traficantes de aspirantes a espaldas mojadas, entre ellos el que las autoridades señalan como "cabecilla", fueron detenidos por Agentes de la Policía Judicial Federal ayer en la madrugada cuando transportaban a Nuevo Laredo, a más de una docena de gentes a las que cruzarían a Estados Unidos.

Los detenidos son Ernesto Sandoval Peña

(a) "El Zorro" y sus cómplices Enrique Flores Hernández y Juan Manuel De la Cruz.

Varios pasaportes mexicanos que habían alterado, con cambio de fotografías de interesados, nombres y fechas, les fueron confiscados en el operativo realizado ayer a las cuatro de la madrugada.

Cuando menos dos vehículos en que transportaban a sus "clientes", también fueron asegurados, en el operativo realizado por Agentes de la Policía Judicial Federal al mando del comandante, Jorge Hernández Pérez y encabeza-

Un buen número de pa mexicanos alterados, f asegurados también po

Desempleo de 50% en Carbón II

1996—El Zorro's arrest in Mexico drew extensive media coverage throughout the Northern Mexico border. El Zorro (left) is shown here with two associates who were arrested with him. This article followed a news release from the federal judicial police.

1997—Receiving Commissioner's Challenge Award from I&NS Commissioner Doris Meissner for Operation Montoneros in Albuquerque. During this conference, A. J. Irwin and I would finish drafting the undercover proposal for Operation Seek and Keep, later described during a press conference by the attorney general as "the biggest ever."

2008—I am in front of the Castillo residence in Compton,
California. Nicely kept home, but headquarters for
major alien smuggling operation, where I spent several
days after being smuggled from Tijuana and then
transported to Chicago. (Credit: Teresa Acosta)

2008—Castillo residence—Rear view of the room I was
kept in along with other aliens when we were smuggled
from Tijuana. I climbed out through the back window to
contact my wife and partner. The room seems to have been
extended since we stayed there. (Credit: Teresa Acosta)

For the rest of the ride, I could look out the back. No one was behind us until we reached the freeway. Finally the car slowed down and we arrived at some sort of apartment building. I could hear Arturo calling me. "Are you okay, nephew? They are about to get you out from the trunk."

I pulled the trunk as tight as I could so it would look like it was locked. We heard the key turn and the trunk rose abruptly. In the bright sun, I saw El Chupon glaring at me. "I thought you wouldn't ride in the trunk?" he sneered. All I wanted to do was stretch my legs. I climbed out and joined Arturo and the eight others who had been inside the car. Two other vehicles that were filled with immigrants pulled in next to us. We were all herded to a second-floor apartment, sparsely furnished and smelling like rotting garbage. Fifteen other immigrants already occupied the main room.

Different smuggling groups seemed to use the place. It was a layover where immigrants were divided up according to where in Los Angeles they were headed. Groups of five and six continued arriving along with their guides. Soon thirty to forty men, women, and children crowded the bare living room, piled with black plastic bags of trash. Two smugglers carried a case of beer each to share. Three smugglers in particular stood out. They looked like they were in the military, down to their haircuts, and their accents were Tex-Mex, which made them distinctly different from the guides and drivers who had brought us in.

"Hey, dude," I asked one of the smugglers in Spanish, "who owns this apartment?" I wasn't expecting an answer and thought that he would tell me to shut the fuck up and not ask any questions, as they normally did to immigrants who dared ask anything.

"Three Chicanos who are U.S. Marines rent this place for us," he responded. To my dismay, he then told me they were from Camp Pendleton, a massive Marine installation in the nearby Southern California town of Oceanside. Their vehicles had access to the base, and they would be transporting our groups through it to circumvent the Border Patrol checkpoint!

That these active-duty military personnel would be transporting us through a U.S. base really pissed me off. Not only were we dealing with lowlife Mexican criminals, but now we were also being aided and abetted by U.S. servicemen who had sworn to protect and defend our country. I couldn't believe these scum would help foreigners evade our laws without knowing their background or their intentions. Some of the immigrants were coming to better their lives, but just as easily they could have been coming to do harm to our country or become involved in criminal activity. The Marines had no way of knowing. Clearly they did not care about the security risk or the damage that could result from their self-serving, anti-patriotic behavior. This was totally deplorable and intolerable.

The Mexican smugglers had no loyalty to our country, but I expected better from members of our military and I knew that I was the right person to make sure not only that they did not continue serving but that they would be put behind bars.

We had been in the apartment several hours when a muscular Mexican with a heavy mustache and a gold-capped front tooth walked in accompanied by two men. The smugglers called him Micho.

"Put away those two cases of beer," he ordered. "Go to the military base and make sure it's clear," he said to one of the men with a crew cut.

"*Sí, sí,*" he responded. "I think our guy comes on duty at four."

"Are you gonna check? We can't take any chances," Micho snapped.

The crew-cut man headed for the door.

It was confirmed that a "friendly" soldier would be on the watch between 4 and 5 P.M. Micho and El Chupon had a brief conversation outside, then came in a few minutes later. I was uneasy with the way they were looking at me. I told Arturo to be on guard. At four o'clock, with military-style precision, one of the Marines informed Micho that their man was at the entry gate. I stared at the son of a bitch. I wanted to make sure I would not forget his face and if I'd had my druthers, I would've just taken that bastard down right then and there.

"All those belonging to the Castillos, stand up and be ready to leave immediately," Micho commanded.

Seventeen of us rose. Six people were escorted outside, Arturo, three other men, one woman, and me. I fully expected to see the beat-up Chevy Nova again but was pleasantly surprised to see a well-conditioned tan Mazda pickup with a camper waiting for us. The woman was placed in the cab and the rest of us jumped in the back. One of the soldiers got behind the wheel. Our driver was Santiago Arana, who I later learned was a lance corporal with the U.S. Marines. He was originally from San Elizario, Texas, only a few miles from where Terrie had gone to high school.

I watched the remaining eleven Castillo-guided immigrants get into a black Chevy pickup/camper. The driver was another Mexican-American soldier, accompanied by an Anglo guy. I was able to memorize the license plate on that truck. Later, when we ran a record check, we found out that a U.S. Army staff sergeant with more than fourteen years of military service owned the vehicle.

Inside our camper, a smuggler gave us curtains to put over the windows so we wouldn't be seen. Just like that, we were being waved through the entrance of Camp Pendleton. So much for base security. Arana drove carefully to avoid being stopped by military police and exited on the opposite end of the base, which allowed us to completely bypass the Border Patrol checkpoint.

We got back on the freeway until we reached San Juan Capistrano, thirty miles farther north. Arana pulled into a busy restaurant parking lot. Soon other vehicles full of immigrants joined us. The military members of the smuggling group had done their part, breaching the camp's security, and we were now loaded into different vehicles to continue our journey. The old reliable Chevy Nova was waiting for us but El Chupon was nowhere to be seen. I quickly got into the rear seat, never wanting to be inside that trunk again. Three good-natured young guys agreed to ride there, and they gladly accepted my cap to cover the hole. They agreed to return it at the next stop.

We drove for about thirty minutes, arriving at the safe house in Los Angeles after 6 P.M. After hearing so much about Dona Carmen and talking to her on the phone several times, I was finally face-to-face with her and her husband, Agustin. Agustin did not give us a second glance. Dona Carmen courteously directed us to a small room next to an alley. Five immigrants were already inside and we were joined by five more who arrived in a second Chevy Nova. Others who arrived were placed in the back of a white Ford pickup and taken immediately to the train station for departure later that evening.

As we headed toward the rear shed, I scoped out the area. I was hoping one of the unoccupied vehicles parked along the street held a backup agent, but nothing stuck out. The shed that sheltered the immigrants was empty except for a pile of thin mattresses stacked against the back wall. The more free space, the more people could sleep there, although supposedly fifteen was the maximum. We learned from some already inside that only ten people a day departed, so as not to attract attention.

After we settled in, Dona Carmen entered and laid down a few rules. "No loud noises. No fighting. Food is served twice a day." The sleeping arrangements had women and children on one side of the room and men on the opposite side, even for families traveling together. Dona Carmen left no doubt that if anyone did not comply, that person would be sent back with her workers the following day. The shed had a small window near the ceiling that opened outward for ventilation. The only door, locked at night with a padlock, led to the backyard.

Sleeping did not come easy our first night. I listened to stories of hardship and deprivation, similar to ones I had heard in Ciudad Juarez. Some people were coming back from Mexico after visiting their families following long periods of separation. Others were on their way north again, after having been returned to Mexico by our immigration authorities. Their consuming drive to get back in was visible in their faces. They couldn't survive in Mexico, making wages of less than a dollar a day—if they could find work at all. One lady with children said she sometimes used her eight-year-old daughter to beg in the streets, and it was breaking her heart. Being in Los Angeles gave the travelers confidence they were almost at their final destination. Ramon, the young kid from El Salvador, departed for San Francisco our very first night. He was excited but scared. He hugged and thanked Arturo and me for taking care of him from Tijuana to Los Angeles. Although I would never see him again, I could only imagine the joy of his parents at seeing him after such a long time. I cannot fathom such a separation from my children or the anguish his parents must have endured during the several weeks when he was making his way from El Salvador to the United States, unable to contact them.

"I could sure use a cold beer!" one of the new arrivals remarked on my second night. I needed to get to a phone to reach Terrie and Gary, so I seized the opportunity to get out. I looked up at the small window and wondered if I could fit through it. "If you guys pitch in, I will go get a case for us," I said as everyone stared in amazement. A number of men pulled out some money and asked how I was going to manage.

"If two of you will bend over, I will step on your backs and go out the window," I said.

Arturo directed the human ladder, and I wiggled through the opening. I landed flat on my back on the hard pavement, but picked myself up and sprang down the alley looking for a store or bar with a phone to call the one person I knew would be there for me: Terrie.

The alley was dark, and I worried gang members or neighbors would see me. I sprinted toward some lights on a corner and was soaked in sweat by the time I reached the blinking neon lights of a seedy lounge.

A lively and loud crowd inside was celebrating the end of the workweek. I must have presented quite a sight—a short, sweat-soaked, breathless Hispanic man walking into a packed African-American lounge. The chatter inside died down as everyone in the lounge turned to look at me. I calmly walked up to the bartender, who was leaning on the bar waiting for me.

"I am a federal agent and need to use your phone," I told him. His reply confirmed he did not believe me.

"I am not lending my phone to any motherfucker, regardless of who you claim to be," he said with a laugh and a bad attitude. He was a big, menacing man and looked like he meant it, glancing around at the customers with cocky pride about how he had just handled me.

I leaned slightly onto the bar as if to say something else to him and motioned for him to get closer to me. He leaned just far enough to be within my reach. I grabbed him in a headlock with all my strength, while pulling my old reliable.25-caliber pistol from my back pocket. Bringing it up hard against the skin underneath his chin, I asked again.

"You think I can use your phone now, motherfucker?" I repeated.

His eyes were bulging like they were going to pop out as he reached for the phone and placed it next to me.

"Now I am going to let you go," I snarled. "Anybody fucks with me, you'll be the first to know. While you're at it, give me a Coors beer," I ordered as I released him from the head hold and placed a twenty-dollar bill on the bar.

The noise in the room slowly returned to a regular conversational level. A number of customers walked out, probably figuring more agents were outside and something was about to go down. Taking a sip from the beer, I placed a call to Chicago, making sure I let the jerk know I was calling collect.

Despite the two-hour time difference, Terrie was still awake. I could almost see her by the phone in our kitchen, as she told me she and the boys were doing well but were anxious for me to get back.

The bartender had no problem with my making a second call. I knew I could count on Gary, regardless of the time, and sure enough, he answered. I let him know I was at the Castillo safe house and would leave for Chicago in a day or two. He asked if he should call the Los Angeles units to go out there the following day, but I figured I had done this well without them, so I said no. There was more of a chance that they would blow the surveillance, figured out by sharp-eyed crooks in the area. In my book, their record was not great. But I was still bothered that they had promised to send support and hadn't.

The bartender was more than happy to sell me the case of beer I needed for the people waiting for me at the safe house. I gave him a twenty-dollar tip, telling him I might be back the following evening and if so, I would have to use the phone again. Returning to the Castillo residence, I walked slowly through the alley in case anyone was outside. I pushed a barrel in the yard beneath the window. Jumping on it, I shoved the case of beer through to the men, then climbed in myself. Going in headfirst, I had to depend on the men inside to catch me as I fell in.

In the morning, a soft voice outside completely took me by surprise. Although I hadn't heard it in several years, I immediately recognized the voice of Maria Gudino. Maria was the wife of a mid-level counterfeiter I had arrested in an undercover sting in Chicago a few years earlier. I had been in direct contact with her when I was ingratiating myself to her husband, Nicky, in a successful effort to get him to sell me counterfeit documents. Before I had left on this mission, I had learned from my confidential informant Francisco that Maria was not only Nicky's wife, but also Agustin and Dona Carmen Castillo's daughter. I knew she traveled back and forth between Los Angeles and Chicago, delivering the collected smuggling fees to her parents, and I had purposely arranged my schedule so as not to encounter her. Now she and her mother, Dona Carmen, and one of their workers were bringing us breakfast. The only thing I could do was grab my completely worn-out, fume-permeated Vietnam cap and place it on my head, tipped down over my face.

I rested my elbows on my knees and put my head on my hands, obscuring my face in the process. Dona Carmen instructed everyone to place the mattresses along the side wall to make room to eat. When I didn't move, she addressed me personally. Arturo told her I had been ill during the night and didn't feel well. He took a plate for me and told her I would eat as soon as I was up to it.

I heard Maria tell her mother that she was going out for a while. I jumped at the opportunity to get to the main residence and gathered the breakfast dishes to take to the kitchen. After I gave them to the worker there, I quickly snuck out to the street to look for backup for me. I walked back toward the shed completely disheartened. Once again I was operating completely alone, even though I'd been promised support by the agency in Los Angeles. I was pissed! My life was at risk and the L.A. assholes didn't care! I couldn't understand their logic, lack of work ethic, and unprofessional attitude. With the chief patrol agent's false sense of having the border controlled and the Los Angeles Investigations Branch's pathetic response, it wasn't a wonder that the Castillos had a remarkably successful human smuggling operation. With this kind of focus, who was going to stop them?

That afternoon, the Castillo mother-and-daughter team walked into the shed without warning to announce who was leaving next. Thankfully, I had decided to keep the army cap on. We were not on the list, and no one would tell us when we would be.

"Just be patient," Dona Carmen advised. "Everyone has to wait his turn."

Finally, the next night, ten of us departed the Castillo safe house. Five were destined for San Francisco and five for Chicago. Three teenage siblings accompanied Arturo and me to join their parents, who had also been smuggled a few years back by the Castillos. By 10 P.M., we were at the Amtrak station ready to board the Chicago-bound train. Agustin had us remain in the truck until the very last minute, then handed us our tickets and told us to board. The Castillos had brought only the five of us to the station, but at least ten to fifteen other immigrants from other vehicles scrambled onto the train just before it departed. Everyone quickly split up into small groups throughout the train.

As the train slowly made its way out of Los Angeles, I found so much beauty in the lights of the city. Looking out the window, I reflected on how much had happened in such a short period of time. I intended to enjoy the forty hours it would take to cross our great nation, a place people were willing to risk their lives to live in. I had just risked my life to stop those who would abuse and exploit our generosity and freedom. I was thankful to be safe and homeward bound. Little did I know I had trouble waiting for me at the train station in Joliet.

CHAPTER FIVE

Takedown in Chicago

ARTURO AND I settled in for the two-day cross-country ride. I would have to be careful on this last part of the journey. Smuggling organizations were known to send "sleepers," immigrants working for the smugglers or sometimes smugglers themselves, to watch over the group so they wouldn't detrain and run off without paying their smuggling fees.

The three teenage brothers who had boarded with us claimed seats near us in the car. They were excited to be on this adventure and were looking forward to learning English, going to school, and joining the U.S. Army. They had arrived in Tijuana with a relative who had handed them over to Castillos' smugglers to get them across the border. The boys' parents had been living about sixty miles west of Chicago for almost six years. They still visited their children in Mexico on different occasions, but had to be smuggled back to Chicago each time, aided by the Castillos.

Arturo and I spent a good deal of the train ride recording the events of the mission. We were twenty hours into our journey when the train pulled into the Liberal, Kansas, station for a short layover. I called Gary from a pay phone to let him know I was on the train and to give him a quick recap of the trip so far. Gary notified Francisco, our confidential source, still working for Domingo Perez, of my impending arrival. Nicky Gudino, husband of Maria Gudino, was directing the operation in Chicago but doing it out of sight and keeping a low profile, necessitated by his recent jail stint for counterfeiting. As bad luck would have it, on August 4, the day I was scheduled to arrive, Gudino informed Francisco that his services were no longer needed, telling him the Castillos and Gudinos had decided to quit the immigrant smuggling business. The reality was that Gudino did not trust Francisco and wanted to keep more of their profits for himself. The operation had been running so smoothly that Gudino felt there was little risk of him getting arrested again. Greed would once again do him in.

This presented a major problem for us. Not only was I soon going to be in Joliet with no way of knowing Gudino, not Francisco, was driving the pickup van, but Gudino would certainly recognize me, as I had personally been the undercover man in the counterfeit sting against him. Informants had relayed to us that Gudino had promised that if he ever saw me again, he was going to get me.

Francisco decided he couldn't take the chance of me getting

into Gudino's van and headed for the train station to warn our agents. As had become his practice, Gudino had arrived at the train station several hours before the scheduled arrival to check the area out for possible surveillance. Not realizing Gudino was in the van, two of our agents, also hours early, parked directly behind it to wait for the train.

Francisco now had to get the attention of our agents while avoiding the attention of Gudino, who would undoubtedly find it suspicious that Francisco was at the station when his services were no longer needed. Walking up to the agents' car was out of the question. Spotting a small gift store across the street from the station, Francisco stepped inside, hoping he could buy some stuff to create a disguise. Quick and clever, he found a white bedsheet and a black bandana. He then carefully folded the sheet until it could pass as an Arab headdress and tied the bandana around his head to keep it in place. A new pair of sunglasses finished the disguise. With his swarthy appearance, he was so convincing that he scared the wits out of the two agents when he approached their vehicle from behind. Unfortunately, Gudino had already spotted the agents and had abandoned the pickup, taking off just as the train was pulling into the station.

Our agents took the three teens traveling with me into custody and called their parents to meet with us at the federal building in downtown Chicago. They were reluctant, most likely scared to meet with us because of their own immigration status, but with their kids in custody, they had little choice.

The long train ride had given me time to write detailed notes, including descriptions of the smugglers, important locations, and each person's participation in the smuggling scheme. Gary and I worked with prosecutors and by late evening had a complete affidavit.

That night, I returned to our house in a quiet Irish neighborhood on Chicago's south side, wanting only to hug my family and indulge in a hot shower and a good night's rest. It was after 10 P.M., and I was exhausted. I was surprised to see a handful of our neighbors in the backyard to welcome me home. Terrie always wanted to make my returns special and had orchestrated the little surprise party. I hadn't showered in days, was a walking ad for the downside of not using deodorant, and was still dressed in the clothing I had been wearing since Tijuana. I hugged Terrie and my two precious little guys, drank a beer, and then went inside for a shower before rejoining the party outside.

The next day, we obtained warrants for fourteen members of the organization, charging them with conspiracy to smuggle immigrants into the country. While I had not anticipated returning to California, it became evident that I was the only one who could identify the drivers and smugglers at the safe house in Oceanside, so I would have to return the following day to serve the warrants.

First I had to locate the apartment in Oceanside. Because I didn't have an address, finding the apartment near Camp Pendleton was difficult. I had arrived in the trunk of a car and left lying down in the bed of a truck with a camper shell. However, I was able to locate it from distinguishable markings that I had logged in my head. One of the vehicles that had been used in the smuggling operation arrived soon after we set up surveillance. Behind the wheel was none other than Lance Corporal Santiago Arana, the Marine who had smuggled us through Camp Pendleton. He stayed inside only a few minutes before walking back toward his vehicle. I gave our agents the signal to hit the apartment building while I approached Arana to arrest him. We both reached his vehicle at almost the same time.

"Mr. Arana, do you remember me?" I asked. I was now dressed in a jacket and tie and looked markedly more official than before.

"Should I?" he answered.

"Yes, you should! You smuggled me through here several days ago," I responded. Giving me a brief look, he pointed his finger at me and said, "Yeah, yeah, I remember now. What's going on?"

He did not get it. "I've got some bad news for you." I told him. "I am a federal agent and have a warrant for your arrest for immigrant smuggling."

The bastard's reply was almost comical. "You can't arrest me. I'm a U.S. Marine."

Before he could say anything else, I grabbed him with my left hand and slammed his face onto the hood of his pickup truck. Unfortunately for him, the hood was hot, and he started screaming from the pain. Squeezing the handcuffs tight around his wrists, I read him his rights.

Inside the apartment we discovered two other members of the smuggling organization, Jose Ocampo and Jose Barragan, both Mexicans in the country illegally. As we were debriefing those arrested, the black pickup used the day I was transported through Camp Pendleton arrived, driven by the wife of Army Staff Sergeant Gabriel Ochoa, who was also stationed at Camp Pendleton. She, too, was read her rights and arrested.

Everyone put under arrest was taken to Border Patrol headquarters for processing. I continued watching the place for several days, but no one else returned.

The takedown at the Castillo residence happened simultaneously to the raid near Camp Pendleton. Agustin and Carmen Castillo were caught completely unaware, and the resulting search of the residence yielded evidence unmatched in any smuggling arrest I had participated in to date. Agents found ledger after ledger with names of more than four thousand immigrants smuggled into the country by the Castillos over a five-year period at an average of $550 per immigrant. Next to the names of immigrants smuggled were names, addresses, telephone numbers, and amounts paid by the responsible relatives in the United States. The ledgers showed dates of delivery, who received the immigrants, who was paid, expenses for guides and drivers, expenses for food, and finally, the net profit for the Castillos.

Seizure of their telephone records disclosed hundreds of calls to Mexico and throughout the United States every month. The handwriting was meticulous. Agents also found a pillowcase containing more than seventeen thousand dollars in cash and handwritten notes detailing how the money was used. Years later, the evidence seized was transferred to our academy for use as a training resource for our agents.

Next, we needed immigrants recently smuggled by the Castillos to testify against them. Gary directed our team of agents in Chicago, and, thanks to Francisco's masterful notes from when he worked for Perez, they easily rounded up twenty-two illegal immigrants who had been smuggled by the organization. All of the illegal immigrants gave statements implicating the ringleaders. Based on this evidence, a federal grand jury in Chicago indicted the Castillos and the other defendants on twenty-two counts of immigrant smuggling.

While in San Diego, I returned my brother-in-law's lucky army cap to him. It had served me well. I don't know if I'm superstitious, but I do know that without it, things might have turned out differently.

Back in Chicago, things got back to normal pretty quickly. Every morning at six o'clock I would head to the gym to work out regardless of how tired I was. I'd play a lot of racquetball with Gary or do some running, as it gave me a chance to think about cases I was involved in. My workouts usually meant we didn't get into the office until eight-thirty. By fate, the one morning Gary and I came in early to review case files for a court hearing, the private phone on our desk used just by informants rang. Informants rarely called that early, and I was unsure what to expect.

"You have a collect call from Margarito Flores from the Cook County Jail. Do you accept the charges?" the operator asked.

My first thought was to just say no and hang up. I hadn't seen or heard from the man we had arrested the previous year for heroin trafficking since his sentencing. How the hell had he gotten this phone number? I had never given it to him. The office frowned upon us accepting collect calls, so when we did, we had to log them in and justify why we had accepted them. It was a pain in the ass. But my curiosity made me accept the call.

I gave Flores a hesitant hello. He skipped the greeting, and went straight to his message.

"Look, I don't want you to think I like you, nor do I need anything from you. When you arrested me last year I asked you not to handcuff me in front of my pregnant wife and kids. You granted me that wish, and I want to do you a favor in return."

After a brief pause, he continued with a startling statement. "You have a lot of enemies out there, Hipolito. I've heard rumors in jail that some people you busted are out to kill you, so you'd better watch yourself. I'm giving you the warning straight up. You were respectful of me in front of my family. I don't want any favors or to be your friend, and I'm not calling you again," he added before abruptly hanging up.

For a few moments, I wondered if he was messing with my mind or if there were actually any validity to what he said. Flores was being held in state custody, while many of the other crooks awaiting trial or sentencing were in federal custody at the Metropolitan Correctional Center. Gary and I couldn't figure out how Flores had learned that people wanted me dead. We notified our management staff about the tip, just to be on the safe side.

After lunch, Gary and I returned to the office and met with Ted Giorgetti, who was now the assistant district director for investigations. Ted's immediate concern was my family. I decided to reach out to Gerard, our informant on the Flores case, and learn if he had heard anything. We had busted quite a number of criminals during my five years in Chicago, so I didn't find it unusual for the lowlifes I had arrested to chatter while in jail. This did not mean I wasn't taking the threat seriously. I started taking extra care driving home, making sure I wasn't being tailed. Gerard and a couple of our other informants weren't able to find anything more than we already knew, but everyone was concerned.

Late in the evening of February 22, I received a phone call from Francisco, one of my few trusted confidential sources. The normal swagger in his voice was not there; he sounded completely rattled.

"We need to meet right away. This cannot wait until tomorrow," he said.

It was already 10 P.M., but I left immediately, telling Terrie I would be back in two hours. Francisco and I met at an Irish pub a couple of miles away. He had learned that a number of inmates at the MCC wanted to have me killed. The information came from a defendant who had posted bond. This released detainee had been privy to a series of discussions held by Nicolas Gudino, Newton Van Drunen, and several other badasses I had arrested. Francisco went on to say that Nicolas Gudino had been in telephone contact with Agustin Castillo, his father-in-law, and that they agreed that the only way they could continue operating in the Chicago area was to have me killed.

Francisco's concern was that the Castillos and Gudinos had extensive ties to organized crime, from Los Angeles to Chicago. He knew they could probably find somebody willing to knock me off for a price. They had suffered tremendously because of my undercover busts, and Gudino was still smarting from the first time I had sucker-punched him by pretending to be his friend, resulting in his first arrest and conviction.

With threats against me confirmed by two sources, Gary and I again met with Ted Giorgetti again. He wanted to know how fearful I was for my personal safety and what I wanted to do. My reply was the same: I wanted to continue with my normal duties and assignments. At the time, Gary and I were deep into another major smuggling operation in Ciudad Juarez that promised to be the Agency's biggest yet. I was blazing the way for us by infiltrating a major human smuggling cartel in Ciudad Juarez that would ultimately lead to an indictment of thirty-eight defendants throughout the United States, and INS Headquarters would have its first-ever national press conference to announce the dismantling of this smuggling cartel.

At the same time, some lesser members of the Castillo organization who had already pled guilty were in the process of being sentenced. It became clear that the Castillos and Domingo Perez were mounting an aggressive legal defense. The decision was made that Francisco was going to have to testify. Unfortunately, that meant his identity would have to be revealed. I was frustrated and heartbroken, because I knew that this development would put his family in grave danger.

Initially, Dona Carmen claimed she had not maintained the ledgers as we had alleged. But a handwriting sample proved her wrong. The Castillos were offered a plea bargain where, in exchange for their testimony against their daughter Maria Carmen and her husband, Nicky Gudino, eleven of the twenty-two counts against them would be dropped. They rejected the offer and instead, in one of the most unusual pleas on record, they pled guilty to all twenty-two counts. Never before or since has any smuggler pled guilty and been convicted of so many criminal counts.

If they thought the sentencing judge would be swayed by their plea, they were wrong. Each one of them was sentenced to twelve years in prison, the longest prison sentence then in the Northern District of Illinois. While I did not treasure the ride in the trunk of the Chevy Nova, I had done what it took to get these criminals off the streets and have them pay for their crimes.

Nicky Gudino agreed to plead guilty to all charges on the condition that the government drop its case against his wife. We declined his offer. He was ultimately sentenced to five years in prison. His wife, Maria, faced a jury and was sentenced to four years in prison, to commence after her husband had completed his five years.

Domingo Perez immediately changed his plea to guilty after he saw the government's witnesses, including Francisco, poised to take the stand. Until then he had been confident that none of the smuggled immigrants would actually testify against him. Perez was sentenced to two years in prison and ordered to pay a five-thousand-dollar fine.

I was in federal court the day Lance Corporal Santiago Arana appeared before Judge Marvin Aspen to hear his sentence. Two "John Doe" Marines hadn't been located, so only Arana was before the court. He arrived in full dress uniform, mistakenly thinking this would impress the court.

Judge Aspen obviously felt the same disgust I had when I had learned that members of our military were involved in human smuggling. In sentencing Arana to one year in prison, Judge Aspen called him a "disgrace to his uniform, his country, and his fellow soldiers." If my memory serves me correctly, the judge told Arana he was a despicable sight. I thought the sentence was a slap on the wrist, but regrettably, this was the first time he had been arrested and a plea bargain had ensured a reduced sentence.

Grace Ochoa, wife of the career enlisted man, came to plead mercy before the court, accompanied by her children and a minister who, in a passionate thirty-minute sermon, informed the judge that Ochoa had found religion and was remorseful for her participation in the smuggling scheme. She fared no better with Judge Aspen, who informed her that he was glad she had found religion, as she could use it while serving one year and a day in federal prison.

The two "John Doe" Marines, described but not named, were issued warrants for being complicit in the smuggling operation at Camp Pendleton. In an attempt to identify them, Gary and I contacted our colleagues at the San Diego Sector and asked them to get in touch with the U.S. Naval Investigative Service and law enforcement personnel at the military base. To our immense surprise, we were told that officials on the base were hesitant to assist in the investigation.

Maybe they were embarrassed, but this was disgraceful. Finally, the U.S. attorney's office in Chicago contacted the Marine commandant's office in Washington, D.C. I was dismayed that two calls from the main U.S. attorney in Chicago to the commandant's office in Washington were needed to get them off their asses and help us with the investigation. It was very disappointing.

That office assured our prosecutor that we would get all the assistance we needed. We got one man, but even so, the third soldier involved in renting the drop house was never identified.

As I had predicted, Francisco's safety had been compromised. He and his family soon began receiving threatening phone calls at their residence. The caller knew Francisco's children by name and also knew the name of the school they attended. All of Francisco's personal information had been revealed during the trial, such as his home address, telephone number, and biographical history.

Several days later, Francisco called me. He was deeply troubled and upset. He told me that several friends had told him that a team of men was in Chicago at the behest of a criminal organization. They had been directed to ice Francisco immediately. So serious was the threat that his children were pulled out of school.

Francisco had placed himself in harm's way numerous times to ensure my safety, and now it was my turn to help him. Terrie and I agreed without hesitation to let Francisco's family stay with us until arrangements could be made for them to safely leave the state and join relatives in California. I asked our agency to help the family with relocation expenses.

Unfortunately, the best our agency would do was provide two hundred dollars to compensate Francisco for his role in what was to date the largest immigrant smuggling case ever prosecuted in Chicago. I was embarrassed at the agency's lack of generosity and personally gave Francisco four hundred dollars from an award I had just received for my work on the case. He was reluctant to accept it, only agreeing when I promised him he could pay me back.

Francisco was a man of his word and several years later, he insisted I accept the four hundred dollars he had saved to clear the "loan."

Francisco's family relocation to California was heart-wrenching for us. The night before he left, Terrie and I had a little farewell pizza party that included Gary's family. By five o'clock the following morning, we were on our way, with Francisco leading the two-vehicle convoy and me following with several of the kids in their 1965 Chevy Impala. Unfortunately, we started our trip in the worst windstorm in years. We had to refuel within the first hundred miles because of driving head-on into the gales. The trip was long, but I filled the hours telling the kids about my youth and regaling them with my nail-biting law enforcement escapades.

After Francisco left, it became clear that my family was also going to have to relocate for safety reasons. After almost six fulfilling, successful years in Chicago, I was informed that Ted Giorgetti had proposed I be transferred. He was grateful for my dedicated service but thought it was too risky for me to continue here. I was being transferred back to Texas, which gave me mixed feelings. My family loved Chicago and none of us wanted to leave. On the other hand, transferring to El Paso was a bit like going home.

CHAPTER SIX

Back Home in El Paso

For the past ten months, I had been involved in a major undercover operation in Chicago disguised as a coyote smuggling groups of illegal immigrants from Juarez to Chicago. The work was thrilling but required great personal sacrifice from my family. My undercover assignments had me away from Terrie and the children for days, even weeks, at a time. Before the El Paso transfer, we received the wonderful news that Terrie was pregnant with our third child, so at least we were leaving Chicago to the joy of a bigger family.

En route from Chicago to El Paso, we detoured to visit my father in Redford. My father was not expecting me, but my urge to visit home was overwhelmingly powerful, even though it was out of our way. We were beat as we drove to the old house I grew up in. My father was plastering an outside wall. He looked at us in disbelief as we drove up.

"What in the world are you doing here, son?" he asked as I approached. My dad had never been an emotional person, at least not one who showed it. I could see though that this time he was choking back his feelings, just as I was.

That morning he had cooked menudo, a popular Mexican soup made with boiled beef stomach, one of my favorite dishes. He asked if I wanted a beer. I was almost twenty-nine years old, and I laughed when I reminded him we had never shared a beer together. We ate menudo and finished the six-pack of beer as Terrie and I happily shared that we were expectant parents again. I still remember his smile. We hugged each other tightly, and I watched him waving from my rear-view mirror as we drove off to El Paso. This would be the last time I would see my dad alive. He died of a heart attack two days later at the age of sixty-nine.

Just four days after our visit, we drove back to my little hometown to bury my dad. For the first time in many years, all thirteen surviving brothers and sisters, as well as my mother, were together in the home where we grew up. With heavy hearts, amid laughter and many tears, all of us recounted stories of our childhood. I was so grateful that I had intuitively detoured home before Dad died.

I reported to the Investigations Branch of the El Paso District Office with great anticipation, happy to be back in West Texas and firmly believing that this would be my last transfer with the federal government. Sadly, I soon learned that my basic plan of working hard and aggressively going after criminal violators was not the norm at my new office. With the exception of a couple of investigators, I found a crew of mostly former Border Patrol agents and immigration inspectors who had transferred to the Investigations Branch to basically retire on the job.

Terrie and I rented a small three-bedroom house in the lower valley of El Paso. At the time, it was a quiet neighborhood with mainly Hispanic families. It was an exciting time for Terrie and the boys since Gabriel was starting first grade and we all looked forward to family get-togethers. We settled in comfortably, eager to move into the new house we were having built.

My office was located in a decrepit building a couple of miles from the main office downtown. The branch office had been moved out there as if it were just an afterthought, and the attitude and work ethic of a great majority of the agents embodied a somnolent "out of sight, out of mind" attitude. A couple of them told me not to disturb their "semiretirement" mode, but, typical of my style, I just couldn't help myself.

Just to get my feet warm, I found fifty open cases in our office files. They were for Mexican immigrants who had been arrested, posted bond, and been ordered deported by the immigration judge but had failed to leave the country. I found it ridiculous that after putting all this trouble into prosecuting these people, we didn't follow through to make sure they had left. They generally stayed at the same location they had settled in and in many cases stayed with the same employer, and no one from our office lifted one finger to stop them.

With only minimal effort, my partner and I traveled to a few towns—Ruidoso, Portales, Roswell, and Hobbs, New Mexico; and Kermit and Odessa, Texas—to track these individuals down. In three days we had located and arrested forty-four of the fifty. Unfortunately, we were instructed to stop our little operation, since there was no way to transport the scofflaws to county jails. We knew somebody was just being lazy though and were not deterred. We loaded up five of the immigrants in the backseat of our little Ford Fairmont sedan and transported them ourselves from Kermit, Texas, to the port of entry at Ysleta, Texas, and personally saw them out of the country.

In another instance, our district director, Al Guigni, insisted that there was no illegal workforce problem in northern New Mexico. He said his agents had only found seven or eight illegal immigrants on a recent sting. I found this unbelievable and challenged him, telling him I could lead an operation into the same area and pick up three hundred immigrants in a week's time. He found my challenge ridiculous but offered to support my effort with whatever resources we needed, including criminal investigators assigned to the area, travel expenses, and transportation for the immigrants we arrested.

The following week we hit numerous construction sites and a meatpacking plant in Albuquerque, and the racetrack in Santa Fe—all places with reputations for hiring illegal immigrants. I took twelve agents, including detention officers and detention buses to Albuquerque, arriving on a Sunday night with our first operation scheduled for the following morning.

Very early Monday, we were en route to Santa Fe, New Mexico, which is about an hour northeast of Albuquerque. We already knew that we would find a large number of illegal immigrants working, because I had surveilled the locations I had intended to target several days earlier.

We arrived at the racetrack in Santa Fe just before 6 A.M., minutes before the employees arrived to tend the horses. By 7 A.M. we had already rounded up between thirty and forty illegal immigrants. We had also gotten into arguments with several of the horse owners, who were indignant that immigration authorities had paid them a visit. One owner threatened to call his congressman to complain about the raid, saying that he had better things to do than deal with immigration. I told him to make sure not to misspell my name when he called the politician's office to file his complaint. The purpose of the operation was to remove workers from their employment and not to target the owners at the locations. It didn't make sense, but it happened all the time. That was part of our field immigration policy, and sadly, the owners fully expected those workers to be back on the job within two or three days.

There was complacency in our immigration enforcement, which continues to this day. Even now, few enforcement actions are taken against employers of illegal immigrants. Immigration is such a delicate issue that nobody wants to tackle it head-on. The problem is that our interior worksite enforcement efforts have never been consistent or effective and this has resulted in uncontrolled illegal immigration. Who wouldn't hire illegal immigrants when the benefits far outweigh the risks? Yet employers would be willing to abide by the rules if we had a mechanism where temporary employees could come in and work if Americans and legal permanent residents were not available.

Next we made our way to the construction sites in Albuquerque. Those raids went down without a hitch. The meatpacking plant was our next target. When we got there, agents blocked the exits while other agents got permission to carry out the raid.

Our actions were swift and effective. Every business raid resulted in numerous arrests. From the construction sites, we quickly visited several restaurants, hotels, mechanical shops, and other companies we had information on. All of them had illegal immigrant workers.

Three days into the sweep, I was instructed to stop because we had arrested close to three hundred illegal immigrants. The buses and detention officers we were using were needed in El Paso. It was time to shut the operation down.

Our operation proved that even with a few agents, we could take effective enforcement actions. I received a call from a congressional office asking about our operation. I had to refer them to the main office. Although the woman didn't give the impression that she had a complaint, an operation like this was never run again in the Albuquerque area while I was with the district.

With my growing reputation, I began receiving requests to help other INS offices with their criminal investigations. In Dallas we went after the owner of a tree-growing company who was accused of keeping illegal immigrants against their will. In Austin I did undercover work on a case involving a minister providing documents to members of his flock. In Miami I infiltrated a counterfeit document vending operation whose clients were mostly Central and South American immigrants.

My agreeing to accept these assignments was not sitting well with our director and, in a memorandum to the regional commissioner, he asked that I not be sent on any more outside operations. He noted that if it was the intent of the service to have me continue in this fashion, I should be transferred to another office.

After that, I stayed closer to the home office to avoid stepping on anyone's toes. In spite of my new caseloads, I had not forgotten a promise I made several years before and a promise I planned to keep—to track down Jose Medina, the criminal who had smuggled me into the country. Seven of his associates had been arrested in Chicago at the takedown, and arrest warrants had been issued on four others in El Paso. Unfortunately, Jose had escaped into Mexico.

Several years had passed and those arrested had long served their sentences and been released, but Jose had not paid for his crime. I was sure he had forgotten about the warrant and was probably back at the stash house in El Paso, which was located a few miles from my office. Occasionally I would drive by the house and watch for smuggling activity or any sign of Jose Medina. I had waited a few years, so I didn't mind being patient now.

One hot Texas Friday afternoon, I convinced a fellow agent, Larry Agustine, to sit on the Medina stash house at 5500 Flower Drive for a couple of hours. I wanted to see if we could run into Jose and arrest his ass. Larry wasn't all that interested but agreed to accompany me if I would join him for a few beers after work. We jumped into one of the department's old four-door Dodge Ramblers and made our way slowly through the neighborhood. I noticed a man of slight build seated on a park bench with a young girl eating ice cream. I remembered Medina mentioning that he had a child.

"Stop the car, Larry!" I directed. I had a strong feeling this was our man. I walked slowly toward him, carefully making sure he didn't see me and take off running. His attention was on a Pop Warner football game, and he didn't even look up when I sat down next to him.

"Are you Jose Medina?" I asked.

"Who the hell wants to know?" he responded tersely.

"I've been looking a long time for you," I said. "Don't you recognize me? I'm the immigration agent you smuggled to Chicago five years ago."

He was stunned.

I had often thought about what I would tell him if we ever came face-to-face. I wondered how many people he had abused during his years as a smuggler but felt no urge to belittle him. Before he could say anything else, I told him he was under arrest and read him his rights. Larry handcuffed him, and we placed him and his little girl in the back seat of our truck. We took off to a place I knew all too well, the Medina stash house at 5500 Flower Drive.

Guadalupe Medina was on the front lawn watering the grass. Recognizing me as we pulled up, she ran toward the car cursing up a storm, telling me I had ruined their lives and that all they were doing was trying to help people. I let her yell until she calmed down, then asked her if this was her granddaughter as I let the little girl out of the car.

"Of course she is," she snapped, pushing the girl toward the house.

We took Medina to the El Paso County Jail. Ultimately he would waive his removal hearing and be sent back to Chicago to face immigrant smuggling charges. He spent almost a year in custody before pleading out to a lesser charge and returning to El Paso. While we were never able to prosecute the vile son of a bitch on the rape offense, I had fulfilled my promise to avenge the young victim who had been so brutally attacked.

No sooner had I arrested Medina than I received information that another former foe, Newton Van Drunen, was probably at it again. An agent in Chicago called me with an address in El Paso being used as a drop point for counterfeit documents that had come from Illinois. Not long afterward, a cache of counterfeit money was confiscated in Mexico. The description of the counterfeiter in charge of both operations left me with no doubt that it was Van Drunen. Although he'd received a lengthy sentence the last time I'd arrested him, Van Drunen had since been released on parole, and in violation of that parole had fled to Mexico with his family, traveling in a bus loaded up with his counterfeiting equipment.

Now my old buddy was again a fugitive from justice and peddling his counterfeit wares in El Paso, of all places. I found it ironic that I had been transferred from Chicago because of the threats on my life that Van Drunen was allegedly a party to and now he was again in my backyard.

I soon learned that Van Drunen was using the alias Guillermo Molinero and his El Paso address was the mail drop for his counterfeit document orders. He was living in Zaragoza, Mexico, just outside Juarez. Van Drunen was now in the business of printing counterfeit U.S. currency.

Because I was now in the Anti-Smuggling Unit, not the Investigations Branch of the INS, I wouldn't be allowed to personally handle the Van Drunen investigation. Although Border Patrol agents could pursue investigations into counterfeiting rings, there was a general agreement that the El Paso

District Investigations Branch would handle these cases. This did not instill a lot of confidence in me, and I decided to undertake a probe of my own, fully intending to turn over any information I gleaned. I asked my then partner, David Castañeda, to help me watch Van Drunen's El Paso address, which we had obtained in between working on other cases. If Van Drunen showed up, we would arrest him. We made contact with a mail carrier, and he verified that mail under the name of Guillermo Molinero had been delivered to the address. He expressed surprise that we were not aware of it, because other federal agents had already interviewed him.

Out of both respect and common sense, I've never wanted or needed to step on someone else's investigation. You never want to do the same thing as someone else and run the chance of encountering each other and getting hurt. I decided to contact the district Investigation's Branch and reach out to my old buddy, Larry Agustine. Larry was the district's liaison officer with Mexican officials, so he traveled into Mexico almost daily.

The other reason I reached out to Larry was more personal. Larry had some serious productivity issues, along with a serious drinking problem, and was in need of a successful investigation to retain his job with the unit. Many times during my career, I have helped agents who were willing to work long hours with me.

Larry was enthusiastic, and we both went into Ciudad Juarez to meet with my source's family and several Mexican officials they had recommended. We also did a number of drives through the neighborhood where Van Drunen was allegedly running his operation. We had a general idea of his location, but not enough information to pinpoint his address. The best we could do was scout the area for a couple of days, and hope to run into him. We had no such luck and without better leads or proof, there was nothing our Mexican contacts could do. They promised to keep an eye out for a large gringo and would also ask their sources to be on the lookout for him. It was their diplomatic way of telling us to take a hike. Even if they did find him, there was little chance they would take him into custody without us being present.

Except for the few agents in Chicago who had worked extremely hard to put this swine behind bars, few people really understood that he was a hardened and dangerous criminal. He loved the idea of being able to screw the U.S. government, although he wasn't as smart as he thought he was. The crook had bought an adobe ranch house in Zaragoza in his wife's name. Then, somehow he persuaded the city to install the heavy-duty power lines he needed to run his printing operation into his home. No one even questioned why the house needed so much electricity, likely because Van Drunen knew what it took to get things done in Mexico—American dollars.

Van Drunen was eventually arrested by Chihuahua State Judicial Police working closely with U.S. Secret Service agents. In his house, arresting agents found sophisticated currency printing equipment and $12.6 million in counterfeit U.S. currency. Van Drunen was now manufacturing more currency than documents. His handiwork was so meticulous that differentiating his fakes from the real thing was almost impossible. The head of the U.S. Secret Service in El Paso stated that Van Drunen was possibly the biggest counterfeiter they had ever encountered. The phony currency provided another source of income for his new dirtbag teammates, the drug lords. Because these scum dealt in cash, they could buy counterfeit bills from Van Drunen and then pay suppliers with the fake money, drastically increasing their profits.

After his arrest, Van Drunen stayed in the custody of the Mexican government until late 1996, when he was finally deported back to the United States through Brownsville, Texas, and turned over to U.S. marshals to finish his previous sentence.

After Van Drunen's arrest, high-ranking members of the Mexican Federal Judicial Police (MFJP), the equivalent of our Federal Bureau of Investigation, contacted the State Judicial Police commander with specific instructions and limitations on pursuing any further action against the master counterfeiter. The Federales were legendary, but not for their success in combatting crime—rather, for their corruption and brutality.

Having dealt with Mexican law enforcement officials, I was certain that a portly gringo like Van Drunen could not have gone undetected without the knowledge and protection of law enforcement officials. The shithead surely knew whose palms to grease.

When he was released from prison, we received information that Van Drunen had moved to Guadalajara, Mexico, the last place we ever tracked him. Even though I didn't hammer the final nail in his coffin, I held a satisfying share of his demise. But I was swept up in a whole new kind of law enforcement action now that I was back at the border. All of the undercover techniques I'd mastered in Chicago would come into play when several of my cases intersected in dramatic and dangerous ways.

CHAPTER SEVEN

Manuel and Sonia Ramirez

"JOE, I LIKE you a lot and I want you," Sonia Ramirez told me as she rubbed her body seductively against mine. We were in a whorehouse bar in Piedras Negras, Mexico, and I was acting as a smuggler named Joe, at the jukebox searching for songs.

I slowly turned and looked into the eyes of the thirty-eight-year-old smuggler and saw her smile broaden. I broke from her amorous attention and discreetly turned toward her husband, Manuel, who was a mere ten feet from us, laughing and joking loudly with his companions. Manuel was with Neto Muzquiz, the designated drug lord of this Mexican border city. They were seated at a crowded table in the middle of the room, admired by a harem of scantily clad escorts.

Muzquiz's bodyguards smiled at me, getting a kick out of Sonia's flirtations while her husband, oblivious to what was going on, tried to impress their boss.

"Sonia," I responded, "I cannot betray Manuel. He is my friend. Besides, he is here in the bar."

"Don't worry," she smiled, "a few more shots of tequila and Manuel will pass out as soon as we get home, like he always does."

I reminded her that I had come with a friend, Gilbert, and couldn't abandon him. Gilbert Wise, my partner for this undercover assignment, was also at Manuel's table, sipping a beer and trying his best to blend in with the criminal crowd.

Sonia was not easily deterred. "I have already called my best friend Gloria, and she will take care of Gilbert," she purred.

Sonia and Manuel Ramirez had recently come to the attention of our office after running afoul of the police on the Mexican side of the border. Manuel and one of his partners had been arrested by Mexican Federal Judicial Police, known as Federales, in Piedras Negras. They had been attempting to smuggle three Yugoslavian immigrants into the United States, which normally the Federales would turn a blind eye to as long as they were compensated to do so. But the Federales were ticked off at the Ramirezes for operating their smuggling ring without paying the "fees." Their arrest also attracted attention on the United States side of the border. Associate Chief Jerry Goodman from the Del Rio Border Patrol Sector was not the typical senior level officer. He was a tenacious, dedicated manager who also liked challenges, and along with Supervisory Special Agent Ken Harvey from Eagle Pass, he targeted the two smugglers operating through his territory. He knew the only way to get the Ramirezes was to run a deep undercover investigation.

"I want the best undercover agent we have on this case," Goodman told our regional coordinator. I was honored to receive this praise from an officer I looked up to and I gladly accepted the challenge.

In Mexico, criminal organizations often pay the police several times more than what they make on their own paychecks, so the temptation to accept bribes is hard to resist. Oftentimes the cartels leave the law enforcers with no choice—join us or face our wrath, otherwise known as certain death. Not only do these dirty officers then take the bribes and protect the criminals, but the rat bastards participate in the crimes. The corruption occurs at all levels of the law, from rural, local, and state police to the very top in the federal police force.

A recent example: In April 2010, all hell broke loose in Ciudad Juarez. Five thousand of Mexico's entire force of 32,000 Federales had been dispatched to Ciudad Juarez to replace the Mexican military, which had arrived there in 2006 as part of President Felipe Calderón's offensive against the putrid, pervasive slag of violence created by the drug cartels. The army was so irreversibly corrupted that the Federales took over the job of restoring order to a city on the verge of anarchy. The Federales were heavily armed and charged with protecting the city's citizens while aggressively trying to stem the daily murder and mayhem of cartel warfare.

Just four months after their arrival, chaos broke out in the ranks of the federal police force when more than 250 officers staged three days of angry protests in the streets of Juarez, beginning with a work stoppage. There was outrage about internal corruption and the risk to their own lives it created. Protesting *against* police corruption by police themselves was truly unprecedented in Mexico. The throngs of officers dressed in blue/black fatigues, many hiding their faces with hoods, accused four supervisors of being heavily corrupted and on the payroll of the cartels. The uproar had mushroomed after a fellow officer, who had lodged a complaint about superiors, had been framed for drug possession.

The street protests reached riot proportions outside the Hotel La Playa, just across from the U.S. consulate in downtown Juarez. Several corrupt commanders kept offices there, and the protesters wanted to physically get at them. Television cameras caught uniformed Federales dragging their top commander, Salomón "El Chaman" Alarcón, out of the building into the parking lot, then attacking him.

The Mexican newspaper *Proceso* reported that Alarcón was the highest-ranking Federale on the payroll of the Sinaloa Cartel, a vicious enterprise notorious for gun-running, money-laundering, drug trafficking, and human smuggling. Alarcón's accusers within the police force said that not only did the scum ignore criminal activity by these bloodletters, but he actively participated in shakedowns, abductions, and even murders.

Other policemen claimed their superiors were so crooked, the slimeballs would plant drugs and weapons on innocent people, and use their government-issue armored vehicles, including some that had been donated by the U.S. government, to move drugs, and jail whistle-blowing members of the force.

The police protesters claimed their commanders forced them to extort ordinary law-abiding businessmen as a matter of course. "We're not all thieves; we're not all corrupt!" screamed an officer behind a ski mask. "There are those of us who *like* our work."

He explained how sometimes convoys of trucks, undoubtedly moving enormous amounts of illegal drugs through Juarez, were ignored on orders of higher-ups.

When the protests were over, the Mexican government promised that all the issues raised would be thoroughly investigated. In an ironic twist of Mexican justice, the 250 Federales who had staged the corruption awareness campaign in the first place were taken to Mexico City to face charges of insubordination.

Had Manuel Ramirez paid off his Federales instead of stiffing them, I may never have found myself pressed against a jukebox by his wife. Our preliminary investigation on Sonia and Manuel had led us to their base city, Piedras Negras, across the river from Eagle Pass, Texas. Like almost every city in northern Mexico, Piedras Negras was a haven for human smugglers and narcotics distributors. Intelligence reports indicated that Manuel and Sonia Ramirez controlled and smuggled the majority of "exotic" immigrants, a term our office used for non-Hispanic illegal immigrants from Europe or Asia.

At the moment, the pair was trafficking in Yugoslavians, many destined for Dallas and New York, where they often found work in pizzerias and other restaurants. Like many well-organized criminals, the Ramirezes were wily and insulated, and it took both maneuvering and luck to get close to them.

In Eagle Pass, we targeted a high-up Ramirez associate, Lazaro Esquivel, the ringleader of the U.S. side of the operation. He was known as "El Prieto," or the Dark One. He was a thirty-four-year-old U.S. citizen and lived in Eagle Pass with his wife and five children. He had two previous convictions for immigrant smuggling, as well as a drunk driving conviction. A hulking, dark-skinned man with black curly hair, he was feared by subordinates who were well aware of his reputation for violence and retaliation if he felt betrayed.

I snaked my way into El Prieto's confidence through an informant, who introduced me as a friend. El Prieto, like so many smugglers, quickly needed to move groups because he always had a surplus of customers waiting. I spent several days traveling with him into Piedras Negras, often dropping in on guides, recruiters, and drop house operators on the Mexican side. Sometimes local cops hit us up for money, which we paid. Doing business in Mexico came at a steep price because everyone wanted his share.

Within a few days, my partner, Gilbert, and I found ourselves transporting a group of twelve U.S.-bound immigrants. Through prearranged signals, a scout let us know when the Border Patrol checkpoint was down. When we cleared, we hauled the two hundred miles to Austin, safely delivering the group to their recruiter.

My undercover work moving illegal immigrants was an emotionally difficult, sometimes overwhelming, undertaking. I knew my motives were correct and I was proud of my natural ability to switch instantly between criminal and enforcer and back again. On the other hand, moving drugs undercover would probably have been less emotionally taxing. Being an undercover human smuggler, while still being a representative of the United States government, complicated the matter. Both sides of the smuggling "business"—the *pollos,* or the consumers in a sense, and the smugglers, the service providers—were engaged in illegal activity. But we had to behave in a lawful manner ourselves or else our evidence could be considered tainted. In the midst of extreme personal danger, we had to be alert and conscious about any behavior on our part that might be read as abusive by the defense in a U.S. court of law.

To make matters more difficult, the dangerous people we were dealing with were not necessarily just the smugglers and the movers. Often they were the immigrants themselves. Most of the illegal immigrants were relatively submissive along the journey, but situations could get rather tense at the drop houses. At that point some of the immigrants would try to run away, or their relatives would attempt to claim them without paying the fee, threatening to call police if they were not handed over freely. On many occasions, smugglers would carry weapons to keep everyone in line.

I suppose that if we had not been agents, there would have been fewer things to worry about. We had to take care of the *pollos* and the smugglers without arousing suspicions on either side. We were compelled to collect the crossing fees for the smugglers, no matter how impoverished the people might be. We knew some of them had hardly anything left. Sometimes Gilbert and I would let some families finagle "discounts" from us if we learned that they had no money for food. But we had to be extremely careful that our underworld bosses didn't find out about our generosity, since this would undoubtedly raise their suspicions.

There were not tears on our parts, but we had hearts and were always sensitive to the plight of families traveling with young children. I was pulled from all sides. Sometimes I had to be a complete asshole.

Undercover work was difficult for any agent. I was trained to play a role and there was no practicing my lines, no second takes; consequences could be pretty bad. Yet one of the most satisfying feelings I got during the times I spent with the immigrant families was when I was listening to their stories, their ordeals, what they had left behind, and what their dreams for the future were. It especially meant a lot to me when they talked about educating their children, keeping them out of trouble, and working hard to one day be an American citizen. That's the attraction that makes our country so great.

Under these trying conditions, Gilbert and I managed our stress and fatigue like the trained professionals we were, and after transporting several loads, we gained the confidence of El Prieto's movers and drop house managers. Eventually they agreed to introduce us to Manuel and Sonia Ramirez, with the understanding we would not cut them out and pay a certain percentage of our take to them. The meeting with Manuel and Sonia was going to require extreme precaution, since we were working without any backup in notoriously dangerous Piedras Negras.

Our introductory rendezvous with the couple happened a few days later, at El Sarape restaurant in Piedras Negras, over a few beers. The Ramirezes bragged about having state and federal Mexican cops on their payroll, yet they complained about what a bunch of asses the police were for wanting more and more money all the time, as if it would never end. Next they briefed us on the nationalities they were dealing with: Yugoslavs, Costa Ricans, Mexicans, Colombians, and Iranians. The meeting with Manuel and Sonia went remarkably well, even though we sensed that they did not completely trust us.

Two days after our meeting, Sonia called to let me know she wanted six Mexicans taken to Austin immediately. She instructed me to go to her house so I could meet Luis, nicknamed "El Diablo," and Armando Salinas, her two main guides. We followed her instructions and punctually delivered the load in Austin, collected the fees and traveled back to Piedras Negras, where we gave Sonia her share of the proceeds. She was surprised that Gilbert and I had not kept a bigger portion of the transaction for ourselves, knowing how other smugglers took advantage at the end of a deal. Gilbert and I liked that we were gaining favor and agreed to join both her and her husband for a late dinner that night at El Sarape.

After our festive meal, Manuel and Sonia wanted to go to Boy's Town to keep the evening going and hear some mariachi music. Boy's Towns were red-light districts that had been established in seven Mexican border cities, including Piedras Negras. They dated back to the days of skirmishes between Pancho Villa and the United States Army, when prostitutes set up brothels near the perimeters of U.S. Army encampments. The remote compounds still operated, providing legalized prostitution and other robust after-dark adult entertainment. Spirited live mariachi music kept the bars and brothels buzzing through the night. Gilbert and I agreed to the nightcap, even taking everybody in our car.

We parked near one of the most popular spots and entered the bustling bar that the Ramirezes had selected. Gilbert and

I were surprised to see a large group of heavily armed guards standing around a table of five seated men, each surrounded by prostitutes.

I quickly learned that the top drug lord of Piedras Negras, Neto Muzquiz, was one of the men at the table. He was Manuel's and Sonia's friend. In the hierarchy of the drug world, drug lords such as Muzquiz are afforded "official" protection, in return for monthly payoffs to government officials, of course. Having this protection, known as having *la plaza,* ensures that the drug lord is untouchable. The infamous drug kingpin Pablo Acosta Villareal, who had "the plaza" in Ojinaga, just across the river from my birthplace, was known to ride around protected by a scumbag general from a military garrison in his jurisdiction.

Neto Muzquiz summoned us to his table and insisted we all sit down with him. Drinks in hand, Manuel and Sonia listened contentedly to the band while Muzquiz and I sized each other up. After a brief private conversation with Manuel, the drug lord decided I posed no threat. Manuel bullshitted him about how long we had known each other, so Muzquiz accepted me. Manuel in turn determined that if Muzquiz thought I was okay, then I was good to go.

One big rule with these drug lord assholes: they mean business and you stay as long as they stay. No one calls it a night until the "boss" decides it's time to leave.

Partying into the morning, Muzquiz and I traded war stories about other narcotics traffickers in northern Chihuahua. I felt at home talking the drug trade because I knew many of the big-time players, by word of mouth or personally, from my work. We ended up drinking and lying to each other until sunup.

Sonia, who had already started seducing me by the jukebox hours earlier, couldn't wait to head home. When the four of us arrived back at the Ramirezes' residence, Manuel passed out, as predicted by Sonia. By that time Sonia had found a female partner for Gilbert. Getting out of that situation took all the wits I could muster.

While Manuel snored from a chair in another room, I promised Sonia that we would consummate our budding affair when we went to San Antonio together in the near future. She promised to go alone, leaving Manuel behind in Mexico. Somehow I made her think it was a better idea to still bring her husband along, assuring her we'd get enough booze into him to guarantee he'd pass out. In the meantime, the information we had gleaned from Muzquiz at the whorehouse that night was a gold mine, a wholly unexpected intelligence bonanza. For the next few weeks, Wise and I continued moving immigrants for Manuel and Sonia, meeting many of their associates along the way.

The undercover operation lasted more than four months, from mid-March to late July. During this time, Gilbert and I stayed at either the Holly Inn or the Hillside Hotel, two establishments way past their prime. The Holly Inn was a longtime fixture in Eagle Pass. It was relatively safe, still used by legitimate businessmen from Mexico and tourists looking for cheap lodging. Unfortunately for us, it was located at a busy highway exit, which we thought might compromise our more discreet activities.

The Hillside was a dump. It was packed with riffraff and oddballs, never mind the odors permeating the place. Immigrant smugglers used the guest rooms to stash large loads of illegal immigrants, and the hotel workers served as lookouts. Because the air conditioners were broken, smugglers had to congregate outside to bullshit and share their war stories. Fist-fights were common between these snakes as they muscled for position and respect. Border Patrol agents sometimes sat in their marked patrol cars in the parking lot, hoping their presence alone would be a deterrent to criminal activity and let the smugglers know they were aware of what was going on. They'd make busts, too, but nothing ever made a difference. Gilbert and I would even mingle with the real smugglers as they gave our agents the finger and cursed at them as they drove away.

"Pinches putos, valen verga!" or "You fucking whores, you ain't worth a dick!" was a favorite expression of the losers hanging around this shithole.

"Don't worry," I would say to myself silently, as if my fellow agents could hear me while the dirtbags enjoyed a good laugh. "I got your back and these shitheads will get what they got coming before long."

We had to fit in with these lowlifes for now but looked forward to the day when we would inform them that we were agents and remind them of the need to pay due respect, since they never knew who might be among them.

In the summer months, my wife and our three children moved closer to my assignment, taking up residence in a hotel in Del Rio, Texas, about sixty miles away. As often as I dared, I'd sneak away from Eagle Pass, usually around 2 A.M., to join them. The dark, hour-long drives were refreshing as city lights gave way to farmed fields, and finally to desert landscapes of mesquite and Texas prickly pear. I'd arrive at the Remington Hotel before anyone was awake, and their squeals of delight at discovering me never failed to renew me. I would grab break-fast with them and spend some time splashing in the pool, then head back to Eagle Pass before my lawless associates found my absence suspicious. I had to finish the job I'd started.

When we finally made our move, forty-one defendants were identified and indicted, the highest number ever on a single human smuggling operation and a record that stands to this day. Those indicted and arrested included river guides, scout car drivers, load drivers, recruiters, spouses of the main smugglers, and most important, the four main operatives running the entire operation.

Manuel and Sonia were arrested after they crossed the river to join us in San Antonio, where Sonia assumed she and I would finally consummate our amorous relationship while her drunken husband slept it off in the other room. Sonia rushed toward me with open arms to embrace me.

"Joe, we made it. I can't believe I'm here," she said loudly in obvious delight. Her unsuspecting husband was a good twenty feet behind. My glare and unresponsiveness turned her affectionate smile to dismal disbelief as I pushed her off, showing her my credentials and telling her she was under arrest.

"Sonia, I'm a U.S. immigration agent and you are under arrest for smuggling," I said. Without shame, she turned her head slightly, looking for her husband to help her, then looked back at me, hoping that what I had just said was not true. Manuel just stared at her. She had convinced him they needed to go on this trip and he had just realized what was going on.

Not only did she not have a clue I was an undercover agent, but she really seemed heartbroken that we weren't going to be together.

It was also time to deal with some of the assholes and their shitty attitude toward *la migra*. One of them was Tony Sifuentes, who had told Gilbert and me that he could smell undercover cops a mile away. He bragged that if he were ever arrested, he would not be taken alive, and it would take two or three of those "bastards" with him. He was about to get his chance. Special Agent Sal Molina, a hulking former El Paso police officer, asked to be allowed to go in alone to arrest Sifuentes while other agents waited half a block away.

"Hey, Tony," Molina said in a gruff voice as he approached the equally huge defendant. "I heard you are not going to be taken alive if you're arrested. If that's true, your time's up!"

The bastard started crying and turned around so Molina could handcuff him. So much for toughness.

Lazaro "El Prieto" Esquivel was arrested at a port of entry during his return trip from Mexico. Both he and his partner had involved their wives in smuggling, and the women were also arrested. Our team at the border also seized ten vehicles.

Our patient, highly stressful, exactingly crafted undercover campaign was well worth it, as evidenced by the penalties imposed by federal judges. Manuel Ramirez received a ten-year prison sentence, while his wife, Sonia, was sentenced to eight. Lazaro Esquivel received the harshest judgment: twelve years behind bars. He had already served time for immigrant smuggling and thought he knew the system. His callous disregard for our laws got him in the end.

Our undercover efforts and successes dealt a severe blow to the human smuggling operatives in the Eagle Pass area. Smugglers, guides, recruiters, and drop house operators alike found themselves serving time in U.S. jails, out of luck and out of business.

The shelf life of cartel leaders or owners of *la plaza* along the northern Mexican border has been and remains today very limited. They can run, they can hide and they can corrupt the system, but in the end they all face a certain death and nowadays, a possible one-way ticket to a U.S. federal penitentiary.

Pablo Acosta, the drug lord across the border from my hometown of Presidio, Texas, was tracked down by Guillermo Calderoni, the top Federale in Mexico at the time, and killed in a shoot-out not too far from where I grew up. The FBI had provided assistance and helicopter transportation on the U.S. side of the border, so that Pablo Acosta and his followers wouldn't escape into the States.

Calderoni, who was allegedly worth more than $100 million himself, was playing both sides and would meet a similar fate when he was shot multiple times as he sat outside the office of a prominent defense attorney in McAllen, Texas. Even if not tracked down by authorities, there are always up-and-coming drug lords wanting to take their bosses out. Such was the case of Neto Muzquiz.

Muzquiz was reportedly shot in the face with a .45-caliber pistol as he opened the front door of his ranch house in Muzquiz, Coahuila, Mexico. He will not be missed.

CHAPTER EIGHT

Undercover Again South of the Border

EVERY TIME I entered Mexico undercover, I was keenly aware that my fellow agents and I were in no-man's-land. Sure, our government would stand up for us if we were taken in by Mexican cops, but they would disavow our undercover status. Of bigger concern was being taken off the streets by criminals or dirty cops and not having the chance to let anyone know where we were or that we had been grabbed.

There have always been friendships and liaison between U.S. law enforcement agents and Mexican authorities, but not without a wariness and distrust on both sides. During my years with the U.S. Border Patrol, it was not unusual to go to Mexico to meet sources and in some cases, even work undercover, without the blessing of Mexican officials. When I traveled to Tijuana for the Castillo case, notification had been made to the U.S. Embassy in Mexico City. However, no one in the Mexican government was aware that I was going to conduct an undercover operation. Even if they had found out, those were friendlier and more cooperative times. There probably would not have been a public outcry against U.S. agents working on Mexican soil. It wasn't until years later that the Mexican government realized how great it played in their own media to decry the presence of U.S. agents on their soil. As a result, they didn't allow any of our requests to target their smugglers and narcotics traffickers, who were protected by payoffs to the same people denying us access.

The well-known smuggler Carlos Dominguez was my primary target on this Mexican mission. He had been allowed into our country as a legal immigrant based on his marriage to a United States citizen. He had no intention of becoming a productive and law-abiding member of our country, as within a very short period of time he was arrested while smuggling a handful of Mexicans from Juarez to Albuquerque, New Mexico. In cases with small numbers of immigrants, it was not uncommon for prosecution to be declined by the U.S. attorney's offices. Limited resources and a general blasé attitude toward immigration enforcement made these cases a low priority. The immigrants Dominguez was transporting were returned to Mexico, and Dominguez was allowed to go free. Within a few hours of his release, he had reportedly picked them up again, and this time he completed his smuggling mission.

Emboldened by the lack of prosecution, Dominguez picked

up the pace, expanding his operation into Central and South America, continuing to keep his loads frequent and small. He was eventually arrested near Alamogordo, New Mexico, as he and other smugglers tried to transport sixteen illegal immigrants to the airport in Albuquerque, where they would board flights to interior destinations. For this offense, an associate and he were sentenced to two years in a federal prison but served less than six months.

Despite this conviction, Dominguez was never deported from the United States and his legal resident status was not taken away from him, although he was now a deportable immigrant. As soon as he was released, he resumed his smuggling operation. Three months later, he was caught hauling seventeen people from Mexico and Ecuador to New York City. He pled guilty, but, unbelievably, was allowed to post bond pending his sentencing. He fled to Ciudad Juarez, where he reestablished his operation in a nightclub, Club Dumas, which he opened on Tlaxcala Street.

Informants and associates we arrested indicated that Dominguez's organization was heavily involved in smuggling both immigrants and marijuana. Dominguez relied on scout car drivers to keep his operation running smoothly, so we began targeting them. Once we had waylaid a few, many others quit out of fear of being busted, too, which gave me a perfect opening to slide myself into his ring as a fill-in driver. Our vamped-up efforts against the scouts at the checkpoint had the side benefit of backlogging groups in Juarez, to the point that Dominguez found himself with almost seventy-five clients whom he was in danger of losing to other smuggling organizations.

Armed with this knowledge, I went to Club Dumas to meet Dominguez for the first time. The nightclub was rocking when my informant, Pedro, and I showed up shortly after 10 P.M. Pedro introduced me to Dominguez. The smuggler exuded an aura of self-confidence—a mafioso-type bravado. We had heard that he was actually rather weak but put on a brave front. He was almost the same age I was, with fair skin and curly, light brown hair. He was fit, slender, of medium build, and very presentable. He was careful with his liquor, and I never saw him drunk. He came across well with women, at least the ones around him at the bar. Even hookers seemed in awe and admiring of Carlos. He, in turn, responded to each one as if she were the only one in the room. His persona was businesslike and professional. He was the perfect CEO of a criminal enterprise, and he knew how to manage and direct his subordinates. Unlike many of his drivers, guides, and recruiters, Carlos was put together and debonair.

After talking a minute, I said I needed to use the bathroom, so I could scope the joint out. I walked slowly, checking the faces of the patrons to make sure I wasn't going to be made. When I returned to the table, Dominguez looked troubled and was very impatient.

He said arrangements had been made for sixty-three *pollos* to cross that night, then they would wait in a field near the Alameda Lounge in El Paso to be picked up and driven north to Albuquerque. I was in luck, I had met him at just the right time.

"I want two thousand dollars to run the road for you all the way to Albuquerque," I told him, much to his surprise.

"Are you fucking crazy?" he asked, as he let out a loud

laugh. "I pay my scouts two hundred and fifty, and they are appreciative I give them the work!"

"That's fine, but I'm not just a scout. Those guys don't use their own vehicles, or pay for their own gas, and can't help you transport some of the *pollos* like I can," I replied. "I have a van, I know the roads, and I can even take several of the wetbacks with me."

Dominguez sized me up, trying to stare me down. I turned around, picked up a beer, and started talking to a scantily clad hooker looking to drum up some business. I guess we had a bit of what's called a Mexican standoff, with Dominguez waiting for me to come back to his table and accept his terms. Calling Dominguez's bluff, I paid for my beers and the señorita's drink and started walking toward the door.

Pedro worried that we had pissed Dominguez off. But I knew what I was doing. "Come on Pedro, it's time we hit a couple of more joints and see what action we can come up with," I said. "Carlos, I'll drop by in a day or two and maybe we can work some business together, but not for two hundred and fifty. I am not going to go to jail for that kind of money."

"Hey, Jose!" he yelled, darting from the club as I was slowly moving down the sidewalk. "I'll go with the two thousand dollars if you put eight people in the van with you after you run the road." I agreed to his offer and started work immediately.

Carlos and I meshed and had I really been crooked, I believe we would have gotten along very well. In this type of long-term undercover operation, you end up knowing more about the personal life of the individual than you had counted on. I learned about his family, his dreams, why he was in the business. Sometimes I ended up finding out that we were very similar, feeling a little bad that we were on opposite sides of the law. I could never accept what they did as okay, but sometimes their justification for it seemed reasonable. Yet I always had to understand that if my identity were revealed, most of them wouldn't hesitate to have me beaten up or even killed.

Dominguez didn't want to cross the group until after midnight. He knew the U.S. Border Patrol agents had a shift change at that time and our chances of making it through were better. There would be a total of sixty-three immigrants coming across in two shifts, and seven vehicles would be used, plus my van. Some of the guides would also be drivers. In total, nine of Dominguez's clan would come across during the night and he, Dominguez, would cross early the next morning and meet up with us in Albuquerque.

Once the group cleared the border through El Paso's port of entry and picked up the waiting *pollos,* they were going to travel a deserted, winding road north through the mountains. The route was popular with smugglers because it circumvented the U.S. Border Patrol checkpoint in Truth or Consequences, New Mexico, leaving only roving patrol vehicles to worry about. Resources assigned to road patrols were scarce, so generally there were only two or three of these vehicles out patrolling at any given time. Once any load was taken down, it would tie up most of the agents on duty, leaving the road clear for the ones lucky enough to follow.

Dominguez told me to come back to the club at 2 A.M., closing time. Once real customers were escorted out the door, Carlos and one of his henchmen locked it. The two guides/drivers who had documents to enter the United States had already returned and proudly announced that all sixty-three immigrants had successfully crossed the river. They were now waiting in a field in El Paso, near the Alameda Lounge on Yarborough Street, to be picked up by us. At the lounge waiting for us were our contacts, ready to tell us their exact location.

At 3 A.M. we exited Club Dumas. Everyone let out an excited shout as we climbed into our respective vehicles for the run. I drove the scout vehicle and headed the convoy of eight vehicles toward the U.S. port of entry.

I had prearranged for agents on the U.S. side to set up a mobile checkpoint on the deserted back road to Hatch, New Mexico, where the smugglers could not U-turn. We also had several patrol units secreted on both sides of the checkpoint to grab anybody who might try to get away. Our plan was to light up the checkpoint, pull over the vehicles coming north, and make arrests. I told them Dominguez was scheduled to come across the next day, so he could be captured as well. Unfortunately, having been hired so suddenly, I hadn't notified the port of entry agents that I would be coming through almost immediately.

"Good morning, sir," I said calmly to an Hispanic U.S. customs officer at the booth. "I'm an American citizen."

"What was the purpose of your visit into Mexico, and is this your vehicle?" he asked, normal, routine questions delivered to most drivers to help gauge their anxiety and suspicious behavior. However, this agent's tone was particularly unfriendly and unwelcoming and he started writing up a slip to have me proceed for a secondary inspection. My long hair and ratty clothes were a perfect disguise but at this hour made me look extremely dubious.

"Officer, I am an agent with the U.S. Border Patrol working undercover in Mexico. I have infiltrated a major smuggling group and all those cars behind me are being driven by smugglers on their way to pick up a large load of immigrants already in the U.S.," I told him. His glare told me he didn't give a shit who I claimed to be. Slapping the secondary slip onto my windshield, he signaled to agents in the booth ahead.

"Please, if you are sending me to secondary, would you at least also send some of the other vehicles behind me?" First and foremost, I didn't want the drivers of the other cars thinking I was in cahoots with the agent and was giving him information on them. Second, I didn't want them to proceed without me.

"Don't tell me what to do, my man," he barked. I wasn't totally surprised by his gnarly attitude. I knew these guys dealt with weirdos who dreamt up all kinds of stories while trying to get into the United States. I hoped I had a better reception from the agent in the secondary area.

But as I stepped out of the truck at secondary, where I had been directed, I couldn't believe my eyes. The same officer who had just sent me for another inspection was conducting only quick interviews with the real smugglers/drivers in the convoy of vehicles following me, and was waving them through without secondary-stop slips. I stood dumbfounded watching the smugglers pass. They were eyeing me suspiciously as they continued on the road into El Paso.

The secondary inspection agent was soon replaced by a supervisor. "I understand you have a bad attitude," the customs supervisor said, as he approached my truck accompanied by several other agents. I tried to explain who I was and the mission I was on, but he cut me off at mid-sentence.

"Unload everything that you have in that vehicle!" he ordered.

By this point, I was furious and the situation quickly broke into a heated argument. I was totally frustrated when they finally let me through. I didn't know it, but the drivers of the other eight vehicles had turned around and gone back across the bridge into Juarez. Fearing I was involved in a setup and a sting, the guides had been directed to return the sixty-three immigrants back across the river as well. It was the only time in my career that I had heard of *pollos* successfully crossing into the United States only to be smuggled back the same evening.

At seven o'clock that morning, I went to headquarters in El Paso to meet Chief Larry Richardson and explain exactly what had transpired at the port of entry. By seven-thirty the chief was on the phone with U.S. Customs Service district director Manny Najera. He expressed his support for me, and Najera stood behind his customs agents. A few minutes into the call, the interagency dispute was resolved. In today's climate, I don't know that it would have been settled as reasonably.

After resting at headquarters for several hours, I was back on the case. I was too close to getting Dominguez to abandon the assignment now. That afternoon, I called him at Club Dumas. His radar was definitely up. His tone was distrustful, and he claimed he didn't have any *pollos* to move. He requested that I drop by the club to explain what had happened during the previous night's run. Those guides and drivers were at the club when I arrived that evening, and looked uneasy when they saw me. Dominguez, at his rear table, viewed me with suspicion. I told everyone about my unfortunate delay at the port of entry but said at least I had not been arrested. Still, Dominquez told me there wouldn't be a run that evening. I sensed he wanted me out of the club, but I wasn't ready to give up and hung around for a game of pool with a couple of the guys. Without fanfare, I left the club around 11 P.M.

Once back on the U.S. side, I called our agents in the Anti-Smuggling Unit to tell them where I thought the immigrants would be crossed, and about the field next to the Alameda Lounge, the usual place to wait for the convoy. Even though Dominguez said there would be no group that night, I didn't believe him.

At 1 A.M., agents from the Anti-Smuggling Unit spotted thirty-five people running across the border highway toward the agricultural field near the Alameda Lounge. The vehicles from the previous night's convoy were also observed near the lounge. The entire group was kept under constant surveillance. Just after 2 A.M., two drivers jumped in a vehicle and drove ahead to scout the road. Only half of the load was on the U.S. side, but all of the smugglers were now on our turf. There was no reason to wait for the remaining *pollos* to cross into the country. Our objective was to get the smugglers.

U.S. Border Patrol Intelligence agent Bert Avila stopped the scout car a short distance from the lounge, while other agents arrested the remaining smugglers and the thirty-five immigrants hiding in the grassy field. Although we didn't get Dominguez that night, I was still planning on taking him down. My identity would not be blown for several more days, when I would be required to testify in federal court against the eight smugglers. At that time they would all discover I was a federal agent, and word would surely get back to Dominguez.

After carefully weighing the risks, I decided that Dominguez was likely desperate enough to work with me. I decided to take another agent, Manny Avila, with me to Juarez. While Manny went home to change out of his uniform and into civilian clothes, I grabbed an hour with Terrie and the kids. The boys were growing up fast and I loved spending time with them in our backyard. Often I'd take them on a run with me through the desert hills around our home, sometimes tying a rope around my waist and pulling their bikes through the soft sand. It was a great workout and we had such great laughs as I struggled to keep going. It sure kept my legs in shape. I told Terrie I had to return to Juarez, but I promised her I would be back by 10 P.M. so we could join friends at a bar for a few drinks.

Even though it was after 7 P.M., the sun was still bright as Manny and I entered Club Dumas. I stood back near the entrance while Manny strode to the bar. All of a sudden a huge blob of a man slammed me up against the wall while another of Dominguez's cronies stood over Manny. I tried to dislodge my chin from under the man's forearm, but the bastard was strong and his huge belly seemed to weigh a ton on top of me. I tried to get a look at his other hand, fearing he had a knife and might stab me. Dominguez walked slowly toward me.

"You fucked us!" he shouted. "Everyone was taken down last night. You were the only one that knew about the load that wasn't arrested."

"Carlos, tell this fucking animal to get off of me!" I demanded. "I didn't know anything about last night. You told me yesterday nobody was going to cross, don't you remember?"

I needed to keep him talking so the big goon couldn't do any damage. Carlos signaled to him and he took his forearm out from under my chin but held me against the wall with his palm on my chest. I wanted to push him out even farther since I still felt a wave of nausea from his liquor-laced breath. I needed to put Carlos on the defensive, to regain control of the situation.

"Hey, I thought you were a real man who took care of your own business. Why do you need this animal to hold me down? Why don't you and I settle it with whatever you choose, with our hands, a knife, a gun, whatever? Are you man enough to take care of yourself?" I challenged.

I remembered hearing from informants that Carlos was a weakling who depended on others to take care of his business, but tried to put on a macho image for his associates.

"Let him go," he told the bouncer. "Come on, let's go to the bar."

My skill set for being believable as a thug sometimes impressed even me. In no time, Dominguez was back under control, explaining that he had lost some of his best drivers and guides in the takedown the previous night; his clients were pissed at him and his other drivers and guides were afraid to transport the *pollos* he had waiting. He had already collected money from some of them, and they were demanding a refund so they could go with some of his competitors.

"I'm gonna take one more chance with you," he said. "But if you truly want to work with me and you are who you claim to be, you have to take this load for me at a huge discount. I really have to recover from this loss."

Dominguez wanted me to put twenty-five *pollos* in my

van. After some haggling, I agreed to take fifteen on the first trip and then return for the remaining ten. Dominguez agreed to travel to Albuquerque in another vehicle to help with the delivery and with collecting the fees.

I found a pay phone in the back of the bar and called Terrie. Using my undercover name, I apologized for having to cancel our "date" that night. Since I wouldn't cross to the U.S. side until 3 or 4 A.M., I wanted my wife to know so she wouldn't worry.

I told Dominguez I was going out for a bite to eat, but he insisted I stay with him until we finished the deal. He didn't want to take any chances with me. After a few games of pool, he told me we needed to go to another tavern to meet up with the other smugglers who would be joining us on the run. The night seemed to be getting better. Dominguez's bodyguard, now acting all buddy-buddy with me, joined us as we left in my U.S. government–owned van. At the tavern we hooked up with the rest of the smugglers and reviewed the plan. Just as we were leaving the bar, several men who identified themselves as friends of Dominguez arrived and engaged him in a private conversation. I began to grow paranoid when I noticed that the group was looking over at Manny and me as they spoke, and I grew even more concerned when Dominguez walked over and asked us to step outside. My gun was in the van and there was no way I could retrieve it.

"Those guys in the bar are friends of mine," he said. "They are negotiating a deal for heroin at another bar and want to take it back to the U.S. with them tonight. They don't want to go by themselves. They want to know if we will go with them, then all of you can take off together."

"Carlos, why don't you come with us to El Paso?" I asked. "We have some girls waiting for us at my place. We can relax and have a good time while we wait for the group to be taken across."

Dominguez seemed to relax. To my surprise, he agreed to cross into El Paso to party with us and motioned for his bodyguard to join us. His only stipulation was that we ride together in my van.

With Dominguez and his goon in tow, we went to a nearby tavern to do the heroin deal. The bar was closed to the general public. It was a drug dealers' hole, dark, smoky, and rank with the smell of stale beer. The small tables were covered with half-empty bottles and ashtrays overflowing with cigarette butts. Everybody in there knew each other, so they were relaxed and wary at the same time. It was hard to tell who was packing, but I assumed everybody had some type of firepower. I had to hide any unease as I followed Dominguez's group to the bar. We sat at one side drinking, while his friends spoke to the men on the opposite side. The guys they were dealing with were dirty cops with the Mexican federal police. There were no introductions, and the four of us downed Coronas while the transaction went down. I was surprised when one of Dominguez's friends walked over and told us they had already placed the narcotics in the car, and that we needed to get out of Mexico as quickly as we could. He told us we would be the lead vehicle, and they would be right behind us.

For the first time on the mission, I was scared. Everyone in our group was tense. I couldn't get out of there and into the fresh air fast enough.

We got into our cars and started for the border bridge. Juarez's streets were filled with every kind of humanity— prostitutes, gringos, natives, drunks, cops, and gangster-looking thugs cozying up to the cops. The traffic crawled toward the port of entry. I was less than two blocks from the International Bridge and could see the lights in the mountains on the U.S. side. I tried to stay calm by playing Norteño music on the radio. In the midnight heat and humidity, we kept our front windows rolled down. Dominguez sat in the passenger seat next to me, while Manny was in the back of the van with Carlos's guard. The drugs had supposedly been placed in the vehicle that was following us. We would not only take Carlos down once we got to the port of entry, but the next vehicle would be blocked in and we would arrest them as well. I was thinking and hoping I would have better luck and be more convincing to my brother officers with U.S. Customs on this go-around. But I would never get the chance to find out.

Our vehicle was stuck in traffic when someone suddenly yanked open my door. With unbelievable quickness, a hand reached across me and switched off the ignition. I had no idea what the hell was going on. A man grabbed hold of my long hair, dragged me out of the vehicle, and slammed me down on the pavement. The goon had an automatic weapon, with its muzzle pressed hard and painfully behind my right ear. I was scared shitless it would accidentally go off, splattering my brains across the road. Everybody was screaming profanities, shoving and grabbing and roughing up whomever was within reach. The other car's occupants were being dragged out into the street, too.

As calmly as I could, I asked the shithead holding me down to pull his weapon back, swearing I wouldn't move. Thank God he did. A number of thugs jumped into our van and started ripping it apart, tearing up the seats and dashboard, searching for weapons and narcotics. It suddenly dawned on me that we had been set up, that the cops at the club who had sold us the drugs in the first place were in cahoots with these idiots who were accosting us now. I doubted if they had even put the drugs in the car. We had never seen them do it. Or maybe they had and were now tearing up the van just to steal them back. Either way, I knew I had to do something fast, or they would certainly find my gun, walkie-talkie, and credentials stashed away under the front seat.

"Señor, tell your *comandante* I want to talk money," I ordered. Deals, payoffs and bribes was the only language the bastards spoke. They didn't give a damn about whether we had narcotics. They wanted greenbacks.

"*Siéntate!*" barked the *comandante,* who appeared out of nowhere. I sat up as directed, and looked up at the potbellied poor excuse of a law enforcement officer.

Knowing they were corrupt but not stupid, I stated, "I am a federal agent of the U.S. government." No one in his right mind would harm a U.S. agent; they would be scared to death of retaliation by the long arm of American justice. "My credentials are underneath the driver's seat."

The *comandante* was momentarily speechless. He walked to the van and pulled a bag out from underneath the driver's seat. I was ordered to stay put while the big cheese conferred with a couple of cronies. They kept looking at me during their aggressively animated conversation, trying to decide what to do. I killed the time stifling stories in my head that I had heard about people who had been taken out to the desert, shot, and buried where they wouldn't be found. I was completely at their mercy, and praying to God to keep me safe. Not only did the fuckers have my gun, but they all had guns of their own.

I could hear Carlos Dominguez trying to work out a deal with one of them, telling him who he was and that his brother was some type of big shot. They weren't paying much attention to him, now that Manny and I had been outed. Suddenly the conversation was over, but we didn't know what the conclusion was. A bulked-out cop shoved the four of us—Dominguez, his bodyguard, Manny, and me—hard into the back of my van, climbed into the driver's seat, and hauled off. I could see they had also shoved the occupants of the car behind us back into their car and were arresting several other individuals that I had never seen until that point. Our destination turned out to be the Juarez jail, a frightening prospect, but better than the horrible option of being driven out of town to God-knows-where and killed.

What the corrupted lawmen would do with us now was the question. A number of cops had sadistically bragged about methods they used to extract confessions. Mexican cops were waterboarding experts before the American public ever heard of it. Truth be told, waterboarding was on their list of *mild* techniques. My consuming dread was that these spineless dumbasses would make us confess to a bogus charge of narcotics trafficking in order to justify locking us up. It wasn't a matter of *if* we would break to their torture, just a matter of what we would have to admit to.

Unbelievably, Manny and I, plus Dominguez and his entire group, plus a bunch of other thug types I hadn't seen before, were all placed in the same cell. It was so packed, all of us had to stand. Just when I thought things couldn't get worse, one of the Mexican cops, who was maybe a supervisor, or maybe just acting like one, came over to our cell and called to Dominguez.

"Do you know who you are with?" he asked with a sarcastic sneer, pointing at me. "Aren't you glad we got you before you crossed? You would be sitting in an American jail if you had gone with your buddy there."

Dominguez glared hard at me, and every single son of a bitch in the cell got behind him and glared, too, eyeing Manny and me with pure venom. It was so tense I knew it was only a matter of minutes before they beat the crap out of us. I couldn't reveal how terrified I was. The cop had deliberately revealed our identities, hoping to get us messed up without having to do it himself. Whether we survived the assault or not, the cops could say the prisoners were the ones who took us down. There was so much muscle in the cell, death by beating wouldn't take long.

Once again, I had to rely on bullshitting, and fast.

"Carlos, what the man said is true. I am a U.S. federal agent and I know you are a resident of our country and you have kids there," I argued with great rationality. "If something happens to me here, I promise you, our government will come after your ass and they will get you and your family.

"Let's get out of this together, and if you make it back to our country, I will make sure my bosses are made aware that you didn't try to fuck us over." I figured that trying to get him and me together in this ugly mess would be as good a strategy as any. Only he had the power to control the pack of thug animals in the cell with us.

Dominguez was considering what I had said. He knew I was desperate, but he also did have family in the United States. His thug posse was waiting for his word to tear us up and shouted at him to do something. With all that commotion, not one guard came around.

Dominguez finally put his hand in the air, and everyone quieted down. I had to keep him talking because I knew this quiet would not last. I had to think on my feet for a better solution.

A guard finally dropped around, but mostly out of curiosity. By this time everyone at the jail knew they had a couple of American undercover agents in custody. Although the guard didn't care about the standoff, I seized the moment. I told him I needed his boss, or else heads would roll. Somewhat deferentially, he agreed to take Manny and me to the man in charge. The head guy on duty was none too happy to see us and viciously screamed at the guard that he should never have brought us in. I felt sorry for the guy, but my own skin was my immediate concern. Right before we entered the office, I heard the honcho talking on the phone about moving us to El Cereso, the scariest prison in the area. That had been one of my biggest fears, ending up at that prison. It was a hellhole, and still is today. As recently as 2011, thirteen prisoners were executed by drug dealers who had been allowed to enter to carry out the bloody massacre. An investigation revealed that even the warden was in on the scheme. From El Cereso, our chances of getting a message to someone in our office that we were locked up were nil. My life depended on being aggressive and convincing the warden to keep us in our current lockup.

"I'm going to ask you to remove us from the cell you have us in," I demanded. "You and your officers have revealed our identity, and you have placed us in great danger and you know what the outcome is going to be."

"You are not going to tell me how to run this jail!" he screamed. "You Americans are always so pushy and think you can get away with everything. You will stay in the cell with the others."

"That's fine," I said defiantly. "But remember one thing, relations between our countries are horrible right now because of the Camarena killing, and someone is going to pay for his murder. If something happens to us in your jail, you need to know that you will be accountable." Enrique "Kike" Camarena was a DEA agent who, only a few weeks earlier, had been kidnapped by state judicial policemen, tortured, and killed while on assignment in Mexico.

"Get your ass out of my office!" he ordered, infuriated.

Manny and I moved slowly back to the cell, feeling our options were running out. Dominguez and his hooligans were back at it, yelling and screaming at each other while they deliberated what to do. It appeared that Dominguez had lost the argument to do nothing to us. Manny and I prepared for the worst and placed ourselves against the wall. It was a fight I knew I was going to lose, but I was not surrendering before taking down as many rat bastards as I could, and neither was Manny.

Just as the yelling turned to physical violence, the guard showed up again and ordered everyone to stand down. Manny and I were pulled out of the crowd and commanded to follow him.

We were taken to another part of the jail, and to our disbelief, we were placed in a cell without having the door closed. I feared the guard had deliberately left the cell open to allow some heavy to come in and rip us apart, or so we would try to escape and they could then attack in the name of apprehending us. Keeping my vigilance up, I observed that when the guard made his rounds, he let the door leading out to the administrative office swing slowly back on its own before it self-locked. I told Manny I was going to take a chance and see if I could sneak into the office.

The next time the guard went past our cell, I waited for just the right moment. I dashed out of our open cell and caught the door fractions before it locked, gently keeping it open with my fingertips. Through the peephole, I could see the guard moving farther away to the other side of the hallway.

Quickly, I pushed back the door and snuck into what I assumed was the business office. Getting behind the desk, I prayed that I could get an outside line to call El Paso. To my great relief, I heard a dial tone. I slowly dialed the number for the field operations supervisor at Border Patrol headquarters. Thankfully, Ray Navarette, a supervisor who knew me well, answered the call.

"Ray, this is Acosta. Please listen carefully," I begged. "Manny Avila and I are in jail in Ciudad Juarez and they plan to move us to El Cereso. I'm telling you in case the Mexicans deny they have us."

Before Navarette could answer, the head honcho, raging mad, barged in on me and demanded I hang up. Tempering my delight, I told him that I had made contact with Border Patrol headquarters, and they were sending someone over immediately. That way he'd think twice about tossing me to the wolves. I also told him the U.S. consulate had been informed.

I didn't know then, but fellow agents in El Paso began to worry when Manny and I didn't come back. Special Agent David Castañeda, my old partner, had crossed into Juarez and had gone to the Club Dumas and found the place already closed. David was a heck of an agent and knew the places where we could likely have gone. He quickly visited each possibility. Finally, he crossed back and went to my house to check if Terrie had heard from me.

My wife sensed something had gone wrong even before he reached her. Seeing David and another agent outside the door so early in the morning, she was terrified they were there to make a death notification. She found little comfort when David told her that they did not know where I was.

David and Terrie didn't know about my call to Navarette. Navarette had reacted quickly to my request for assistance, notifying the senior staff and Chief Richardson of my crisis. Intelligence officer Bert Avila, who was our liaison officer with Mexican law enforcement officials, immediately called a number of his high-level contacts in Ciudad Juarez to ask for their intervention. Bert knew that time was of the essence and contacted the State Department. Within half an hour, Avila and Imogene Iwakara, an officer from the State Department, were on their way to Juarez to secure our release.

Arriving at the jail, Avila asked to speak to the individual in charge. When he was refused, he simply walked into the head guy's office and told him that the U.S. government knew they had us at that facility and that he and Imogene would not leave until they saw us. The Mexican officials denied we were in their custody. For several hours, Avila and Iwakara stood guard at the facility as the appropriate notifications were made to our headquarters, the U.S. consulate in Ciudad Juarez, and the U.S. Embassy in Mexico City.

Had all this not happened, I don't know that the outcome of my detention would have been resolved as uneventfully as it was. Eventually Manny and I were released, but Dominguez and his party also got out. Neither he nor any of his goons were charged with any type of criminal activity. The official version from the Mexican government about our arrest and release was that all of those in Dominguez's party, including Manny and me, had been detained for drinking in public. They said nothing about the narcotics. In return for our not contradicting their version, the Mexican government agreed to return my credentials, weapon, walkie-talkie, and our U.S. government van. Manny and I were happy to agree to that, and by the following evening, we were transported back to U.S. Border Patrol headquarters.

Eight defendants arrested on the U.S. side were convicted on immigrant smuggling charges. Dominguez continued with his operation on the Mexican side, while outrageously wanting to file a complaint against us for what he termed as a kidnapping attempt against him. He was not shy about going to the press with his claims. One of the newspapers reported our "indignant" actions in violating Mexican sovereignty while working undercover in Mexico. Ultimately he reentered the United States and was arrested again for immigrant smuggling, served prison time in the United States, and was officially deported. I would not be surprised if he is here again, but wherever he is, it does seem likely that he is in gainful and respectable employment.

Notwithstanding the outcome of my dogged pursuit of Dominguez, two years with the U.S. Border Patrol's Anti-Smuggling Unit in El Paso had been enough for me to turn the office around. We had made great progress and busted many significant criminal enterprises. I was ready for a change, and Brownsville, eight hundred miles east, was my next destination. I was slated to be the supervisory special agent in charge of the Anti-Smuggling Unit there. This would be my first management position, and I had my work cut out for me.

At the time of my assignment, Matamoros, across the border from Brownsville, was one of the most dangerous, crime-infested cities in Mexico. Even though we were small in number, our office managed to lead the entire nation in criminal prosecutions and convictions during my two-year tour as leader of the Brownsville Station's Anti-Smuggling Unit. I had been a member of the Border Patrol for fourteen years when I learned I had been selected as Assistant Officer in Charge in Manila, Philippines, a small sub-office of the Bangkok District. Initially skeptical, my wonderful family was soon excited at the prospect of moving across the ocean.

The Philippines was a unique assignment. The diversified workload was exciting and challenging. Illegal immigration issues in the Philippines were different than they were in Mexico. Both Mexicans and Filipinos were willing to risk their savings and their lives for the same reasons: getting away from dire poverty and making a better life for themselves. However, to get from the Philippines to their country of choice, Filipinos needed transportation beyond what a Mexican coyote could provide: they needed documentation. So most of the illegal activity revolved around document fraud. Even if visas were obtained properly, they were for fraudulent reasons.

Terrie and my children made significant sacrifices for my career, and I was grateful. My children seemed to thrive in Manila. They attended the International School Manila (ISM), played sports and participated in athletic events in Taipei, Hong Kong, and Bangkok. We met people from the Philippines and other countries who remain friends to this day. But when an opportunity arose at the U.S. Consulate in Monterrey, Mexico, to be the Officer in Charge of the INS Office, I accepted. In August 1994, we left the Philippines for Mexico.

CHAPTER NINE

El Zorro

MONTERREY WAS IN a gorgeous area in the mountains of
northeast Mexico one hundred miles from the Texas border.
Driving into the city from the north, Terrie and I were amazed
by the sight of it. I was excited because this would be my first
post where I would actually be stationed in Mexico. We came
with mixed emotions. We were excited to be in a Spanish-
speaking environment yet we were apprehensive, concerned
for our family's safety. I had already done a lot of undercover
work in Mexico and had put many of its citizens in jail, so
I knew the risks. At the same time, I was thrilled that smugglers and criminals who thought they could avoid U.S. justice
by staying south of the border would now be in my sights. I
would be in their backyard.

Monterrey, which is Mexico's third-largest metropolitan area, is surrounded on all sides by the Sierra Madre Mountains, in a setting of spectacular natural beauty. The older part of town still had the elegant architecture of colonial days, but as the city grew, the wealthy, progressive-minded inhabitants turned it into a sleek, modern metropolis with museums, theaters, sports venues, hotels, and restaurants. Mexican and international corporations alike filled the floors of its modern skyscrapers.

My family and I arrived in Monterrey just in time to witness the monarch butterfly migration, one of the most extraordinary and significant biological events on earth. Three hundred million butterflies, having traveled more than three thousand miles, winter in Mexico at their own butterfly biosphere preserve just outside the city. Terrie and I had migrated to the area as well, but our journey had taken us 8,500 miles, all the way from a five-year tour in the Philippines. While there, we discovered corruption within the ranks of the U.S. government, resulting in removal of several officials at the U.S. Embassy in Manila. It was one of the busiest posts of any foreign State Department office. One of my crowning achievements in the Philippines was coordinating the naturalization program for the Philippines' loyal, heroic World War II veterans. Through my initiative, more than seven thousand of these forgotten heroes became U.S. citizens. It was decades overdue, but no less deserved.

Our new post was about two hundred miles west of Brownsville and 150 miles south of Laredo, nowhere near a border but connected to it by well-maintained, expensive toll roads. The modern highway system gave both aboveboard travelers and underhanded smugglers easy access to the ports of entry into the United States.

Within weeks of my arrival, I was in hot pursuit of one of the most successful backstreet human smugglers in all of Mexico, the legendary Ernesto Sandoval-Pena, aka El Zorro, "the Fox." This coward had stopped coming to the United States in an attempt to distance his criminal activity from the law, but he was going to learn that American justice was far-reaching.

El Zorro had been the target of investigations at the Monterrey office as well as INS offices in the States for years. He wasn't an imposing man, but he was respected and carried himself with an air of authority, an invaluable trait in the underworld. He was sly as a fox, thus the moniker. He had extensive influence in Mexico through corrupt Mexican officials, and he allegedly had several U.S. immigration inspectors in his pocket at our port of entry in Laredo, Texas.

El Zorro pretended to be a businessman, posing as the owner of an automotive repair and body shop as well as running some type of office service from his residence. His real occupation was illegally transporting hundreds of immigrants a month. The automotive shop provided him with the vehicles he needed to bring the large number of clients to their visa interviews at the U.S. consulate in Monterrey or to their entry points along the U.S. border. Civic minded, he sponsored one of the Nueva Rosita baseball teams, which included several of his drivers and associates.

His services were so in demand that he needed two full-time secretaries to keep track of the bookkeeping. Clients regularly waited two weeks for an appointment. He ran the business openly, meeting with clients in the living room of his stucco house in the coal-mining town of Nueva Rosita, one hundred miles west of Monterrey. There was even a hotel in town that catered solely to his clientele. It seemed like an unlikely place from which to operate such a successful human smuggling enterprise. However, it was actually ideal. El Zorro was so confident that his business wouldn't be busted that he took no precautions to keep it under wraps. In fact, he was revered as a local hero, giving poor, desperate people a chance at a better life in the United States.

His operation was simple. Plan A was to try to get legitimate visas for his clients. Getting a visa didn't really mean the applicant was honorable and eligible; anybody could apply. The interviewing officers, who only had two minutes or less to interview a candidate, had to make snap decisions on whether to approve or reject an application. The results were similar to flipping a coin, no insult to the interviewers intended. El Zorro knew the odds, and as a result, visas were granted to half of his customers. The other half was taken back to Nueva Rosita for Plan B.

El Zorro had a stash of tampered documents and counterfeit visas that could be used by his clients if they weren't issued an authentic visa. The fakes were so good, they could be presented at our ports of entry in Laredo, Del Rio, and Eagle Pass, Texas, with almost certain success. Once the traveler was safely across, the documents were collected by El Zorro's guides or drivers and brought back to him so they could be photo-substituted and doctored for reuse. Under the slim chance that the fake did not work, El Zorro would have his clients smuggled the traditional way, across the Rio Grande. In the end, he was close to 100 percent successful in getting his people into the United States.

El Zorro had another advantage going for him: his wife, Alma. She was his business partner, but in the legitimate world, she was an employee at the Mexican social security office. Informants indicated that in her position, she had access to documents that clients needed to get genuine visas at the U.S. consulate in Monterrey.

Prior to my arrival, a task force had already been assembled, and an investigation into El Zorro's activities was under way. The plan was to arrest him when he crossed into the United States with one of his loads. We had successfully infiltrated his operation, and one of our informants had secured an appointment to be smuggled into the States.

The problem was that someone within our ranks had gotten to El Zorro and tipped him off. Agents had actually observed him walking to the middle of the International Bridge in Laredo, Texas, where he met with one of our U.S. immigration inspectors before turning around and walking back into Mexico.

I decided my best approach was to go undercover and visit his Nueva Rosita operation. Finding it was easy. Everybody in town knew where he lived. The house was a short distance from the hotel where his clients stayed, and the foot traffic between the two went on day and night. The house, in a middle-class neighborhood, was well kept and inconspicuous. It was raised on a cement foundation and coated with white plaster. Clients climbed up and down the stairs to the front door so regularly that it was rarely closed. Cigarette-smoking peasants stood in the front yard, waiting for their turns.

After three days of watching, I knew I could go in as a hopeful traveler. I walked inside to what would have been a living room had the house been residential. Instead it was a waiting room in a business office, with a small desk for the secretary and four or five inexpensive chairs for the clients. Nobody had to wait long. The secretary told hopefuls to check in at the hotel down the road and wait for further instructions.

Even though I didn't have a credible referral, the young woman who greeted me directed me to get a room and wait. It would be several days before someone would get back to me, she said.

No one appeared disturbed by my visit, so I watched the house for several more hours before returning to Monterrey to strategize with my team.

Next, I enlisted another agent from the Monterrey office, Alfonso Pineda, to join me on several surveillance missions in Nueva Rosita to track El Zorro as he moved his clients to the Mexican border city of Nuevo Laredo in preparation for crossing. An informant told us that El Zorro had been warned that we were watching him, but he didn't seem extraordinarily cautious. He had already decided to never set foot on U.S. soil again, and he wasn't concerned about being tailed inside Mexico. He fearlessly escorted his clients as far as Nuevo Laredo, where he turned them over to guides and drivers to continue their journey into the United States.

We needed a new strategy to take him down. I recommended trying to have El Zorro arrested in Mexico. He would never expect us to take a stab at prosecuting him on his home turf. It wouldn't be easy. We would have to convince Mexican law enforcement officials to cooperate in arresting their own man, even though many already knew of El Zorro's criminal activities and might even be recipients of payoffs from him. An even bigger obstacle was keeping El Zorro in the dark about what we were planning. He had close associates on both sides of the border, and it would have been naïve to think that word would not get back to him. This meant that his criminal gang would be even more vigilant of individuals trying to infiltrate his group. Yet I counted on his greed. This is how he made his living and he was not about to quit.

In a cooperative effort, we met with agents of the Procuraduría General de la República (PGR, the Mexican attorney general's department), assigned to the Mexican consulate in San Antonio to ask for their assistance in targeting El Zorro in Mexico. They said they needed altered Mexican passports and sworn statements from witnesses, which we provided. But we hit a wall when the PGR didn't follow through with their promise to forward the evidence to officials at their headquarters in Mexico City.

Opposition was not limited to the Mexican bureaucrats. A number of stateside officers wanted only to continue with their original plan—to capture El Zorro in the United States for prosecution here. One supervisor in Eagle Pass was particularly turned off and refused to even entertain my idea of pursuing El Zorro through the Mexican legal system. He was a real asshole, a know-it-all, even though he'd never even participated in a single undercover operation in his career. He was the epitome of someone who rises through the ranks kissing ass and ultimately getting promotions without having done anything to deserve them. Hoping he'd see my point, I invited him to join us on the Mexican side. When he agreed, we left the prosecutor's office in teams to surveil and take down El Zorro, me on one team and him on another. I became concerned when he didn't answer any of my radio calls in the field. I didn't see the bastard again until the next day, on the U.S. side. Apparently he had come up with a lame excuse to return to the American side so he wouldn't have to travel deep into El Zorro's territory. It was a chickenshit move.

El Zorro was a bold operative but didn't display a cocky, in-your-face attitude. Of medium build, a receding hairline, and a boyish face, he ran his organization with a tight grip. The desolate location of Nueva Rosita provided him yet another advantage of intercepting anyone trying to cut into his territory. He had been in business for fifteen years and knew what he was doing. In all likelihood, he would continue for another fifteen or more if I couldn't make a case against him.

In Monterrey, our agency at the U.S. consulate had two excellent Foreign Service national investigators, Jorge Garibay and Mauro Huerta. The two men had extensive contacts throughout the region. Foreign Service Nationals, or FSNs as they are referred to, are foreign locals who become U.S. employees at our diplomatic missions worldwide. The positions are coveted and the great majority of FSNs are very hardworking and extremely loyal to our country.

After fifteen years of service, they can apply for special visas to immigrate to the United States with their families if their service is determined to have been exceptional. Many avail themselves of this opportunity. American personnel come and go through tour rotations while FSNs provide the continuity and support needed for everyday operations. I was fortunate to have these two solid FSNs working under me. They in turn were enthusiastic about being involved in "sensitive" criminal investigations since their talents and participation had been restricted by previous office heads in Monterrey. They appreciated the trust and faith I placed in them.

Huerta was a particularly sharp criminal lawyer who knew Mexican law well. He and Garibay were able to find legal grounds to prosecute El Zorro in several jurisdictions in Mexico. During his many years in the business, El Zorro had made a practice of using different entry points at the border. Doing so made his operation look smaller at each location and attracted less attention from law enforcement officials on both sides of the border. To our advantage, it gave us different areas of opportunity where violations were occurring and through which we could seek prosecution.

Pineda, Huerta, Garibay, and I made a great team. Again, this was a case where my subordinates believed in my leadership and the mission. These guys were not only loyal, they were willing to do whatever it took and devote the time needed to accomplish what officials on both sides of the border said couldn't be done—putting El Zorro behind bars.

Mexican prosecutors weren't interested. For the first round of meetings, we were either stood up or made to wait for hours. If they did show up, they would tell us we were in the wrong jurisdiction and direct us somewhere else. While we were en route to "somewhere else," somebody would call the office we were headed for and warn them that we were coming and tell them what we were seeking. It pissed me off that many times we would arrive and the prosecutor would pull a law book from his shelf to read the section of the law that prevented them from going after El Zorro. Not caring to establish a friendship, on numerous occasions I stopped them in the middle of the reading and asked them to find a section of law that could be used to prosecute the turkey. That generally ended the meeting. While I had not gotten the results I wanted, I at least felt I had gotten the message across that they were not succeeding in bullshitting me.

In Nueva Rosita they blew us off. In Nuevo Laredo, federal judicial police were more interested in protecting their turf and collecting from the drug traffickers and human smugglers than taking down El Zorro. The prosecutors in Nuevo León, Acuña, Saltillo, and Sabinas were equally dismissive. No matter what plan we came up with to make them hear us, they gave us a load of crap and wouldn't cooperate.

The long drives between prosecutors' offices were tiring and always caused us concern for our safety. We were making more and more enemies, and everybody now knew what we were up to. We were foreign agents, and therefore completely unarmed, in the pits of Mexico. We had no communication, no armor-plated vehicle, and no backup. We were in the heart of danger, drug lords and cartel thugs were everywhere. El Zorro was a legend and a hero in these parts, and we were fucking with him.

On many occasions, I'd pretend to be staying overnight to try to develop a cohesive working relationship with the law enforcement leadership and woo them to my side to assist us. Like a businessperson anywhere, I'd wine and dine them for several hours. I'd use my wit, charm, and balls to persuade them and make them think I wasn't afraid. Truth was, I was very aware of what some of these guys were capable of and I needed to be vigilant for my well-being. Call it a healthy fear, but it kept me going, and I have no doubt that following my intuition in my many years of working undercover kept me alive.

These guys all knew where I was staying and would have taken my life for a nickel. There was no way I would spend the night in their turf, even though I had a room. After dinners, I'd go back to my lodging, then quietly slip out the back and drive out of town. I didn't want to be the victim of some type of "accident."

The only prosecutor's office left on my list was in Piedras Negras, the dangerous border town where I had successfully infiltrated the smuggling operation of Sonia and Manuel Ramirez and had encountered Neto Muzquiz, the local drug lord. I briefed Benito Villareal, the young federal prosecutor in charge of that office, and hoped for the best. He was my last chance.

Villareal was originally from Monterrey and a member of one of the wealthier families in that city. He patiently listened to my presentation without making a single note. He gave me his complete attention. My hopes were raised when he asked if I would join him for lunch at a nearby restaurant. Nothing about the case was mentioned during the meal. When we returned to his office, Benito finally gave me his opinion.

"Look, this guy is transporting Mexicans to the border. There is no violation there and while I understand the concerns of the U.S. government, I don't believe I can help you," he said.

During the brief period we had spent together, I felt comfortable in pushing the issue with him. "Benito, give me just a little bit more of your time and listen to me once again. There has got to be someone in Mexico who wants to do the right thing," I told him. "Mexican passports are being altered and used by individuals that might or might not be citizens of Mexico. Doesn't anybody in this country give a shit?"

He was surprised at my comment and for a moment I thought he was going to ask me to leave, but instead he asked that we talk inside. Making sure I didn't cross the line, I went through the entire case again. He showed renewed interest in pursuing El Zorro when I told him that the case had reached the attention of U.S. attorney general Janet Reno's office and they had a strong interest in the outcome of the matter. It might have been a bit of a stretch on my part, but then again we had submitted an undercover proposal to the Department of Justice in Washington, D.C., and had received their concurrence for it. It didn't hurt that Janet Reno *was* in fact coming to Mexico, but not about El Zorro. I was certainly glad I had piqued his interest. He assured me that regardless of who was protecting El Zorro, his office would prosecute him if there were violations of Mexican law.

It took a lot of urging but ultimately Benito allowed us to send in a couple of informants to obtain counterfeit documents from El Zorro. However, he said that once we had the evidence in hand, El Zorro would have to be arrested and prosecuted right away. Benito wanted to get it done immediately and move forward before anybody could intercede on El Zorro's behalf. He said it was the only way. If we waited, he would surely change his tactics. No doubt word would get back to him, and the bastard would have the time to pay Mexican officials to protect him.

Back in Eagle Pass, I briefed the antismuggling staff, and by

4:30 A.M. the following morning, we were all meeting in the parking lot of PGR headquarters in Piedras Negras. The magnitude of this meeting in a dimly lit area outside a Mexican law enforcement agency did not go unnoticed by me. Benito and I were doing a joint briefing for American and Mexican officers in their territory, pairing law enforcement officers from two different countries.

There was no way I would have our officers unarmed on a raid in Mexico but I did ask them to conceal their weapons. I have no doubt that Benito was aware of our intentions to be armed and he completely understood, but I didn't want to place him in a difficult position by telling him we were armed. We had no idea what we would encounter once it went down. I was not too worried about El Zorro. I was more concerned about some of his subordinates, several of whom had previously been arrested and served time in the United States.

By 6 A.M. we had both the hotel and El Zorro's residence in Nueva Rosita under surveillance. Some of our officers were not familiar with the area so I suggested that we pair up for safety and expediency. I had an ulterior motive—to prevent Mexican officers from warning El Zorro, since they had not learned of what our plans were until this early morning briefing. His officers were not pleased, which worried me, as we would be traveling through desolate Mexican backcountry. I felt certain that the agents under Benito's leadership would perform as they had been instructed but I didn't have complete trust in every single one of them. All it took was one to warn our targets and things could get awfully messy. In my mind, no case has ever been worth the life of one of our agents.

Everybody was extremely tense during the ride to Nueva Rosita. An hour and a half later, we all regrouped near El Zorro's residence. Using walkie-talkies, Benito and I instructed agents in other vehicles to park several blocks from the house. El Zorro might have been confident that no one would bother him in his backyard, but he was no fool, and vehicles with two strange men would undoubtedly get his attention.

Twenty-eight clients were outside, next in line to depart for the border. Once again we were breaking ground in our efforts to thwart illegal immigration and catch the smugglers behind it. American agents for the first time were watching a group organize at the base of operations of a major criminal in a foreign country.

We could see El Zorro and several individuals who appeared to be his confidants as they gave last-minute instructions to the men and women congregated in front of his residence. El Zorro might have seemed confident, but we could tell from the short distance from where we were watching that many in the group were not. They might have been embarking on a new adventure, but in reality they were leaving their homes and families in search of a new life. I had seen those looks before.

At 9:30 A.M., they loaded into four different vehicles. El Zorro and his group were quick and decisive as they gave instructions to their *pollos*. Pointing to different vehicles, they shouted instructions so that their clients understood exactly where they wanted them to go and they would not lose any time. El Zorro and his smugglers were making sure their clients knew exactly who was in charge and no deviation was acceptable. We could see the meekness in the group as they submissively moved toward the vehicles. We had to react in a similar manner, but with the Mexican Federales.

"They are moving out," I told Benito. "We need to make sure your officers know which vehicles to follow and what to do once we get outside Nueva Rosita." His look told me he understood and although he was confident, I could tell that Benito was hesitant. This was new territory for him as well and I am sure he was thinking of the possible consequences.

Forcefully giving orders through his radio, he reminded his team of the instructions they had received at PGR headquarters in Piedras Negras. Notwithstanding his self-assurance, he left no doubt in his instructions that he expected success. Each of the vehicles was pursued by a PGR agent and one of our own. Outside the city limits, one of the supervisors passed the order through his radio to begin stopping the vehicles. These Mexican cops didn't need or use red flashing lights to pull the vehicles over. Simply pulling alongside the vehicle, they startled each of the drivers.

"Pull your ass over, you son of a bitch!" one of the Federales yelled at one of the men.

They had no reason *not* to pull over, since they assumed they were simply being shaken down. El Zorro would pay the *mordida,* or bribes, and they would continue with their journey.

But this was not business as usual. Unfortunately, the lead vehicle, a Suburban, kept on going. The driver of the PGR vehicle designated to stop it claimed that he misunderstood and stopped with the second vehicle in the procession instead. He was dispatched to try to catch it but returned a few minutes later, stating that it appeared the vehicle had turned off from the main road. Despite our best efforts and Benito's insistence, one of El Zorro's men had still gotten one over on us.

We set up yet another convoy and started driving back to Piedras Negras. Benito was obviously pissed at what had happened with the Suburban but tried to play it cool with me. We stayed close behind the group so that we could observe them.

I had two of our officers back at PGR headquarters, and along with several Mexican officers, they started interviewing the passengers. I was pleasantly surprised with those in custody. Two of his main lieutenants helping him were with the group, coordinating the operation. In addition, there were two veteran guides who were to lead a group to San Antonio, and two other criminals who were escorting part of their group to the Laredo port of entry, where they planned to get entry permits. We also had one of their regular drivers, but the biggest prize was Ernesto Sandoval-Castaneda—El Zorro.

After fifteen years, we finally had the bastard in custody in his own backyard, his own country. The Lone Ranger—that would be me—had ridden into Mexico to conquer El Zorro, the smuggling imposter who had given our mythical hero's namesake a bad rap.

Arresting El Zorro and his cohorts was one thing, prosecuting them was another, and we faced another battle in getting Benito Villareal to follow the case through. Mexican law requires that individuals arrested be charged with an offense within thirty-six hours. Some of the PGR agents were clearly not pleased with the detention of El Zorro. In fact, it seemed that they were waiting for us to leave the detention center so they could come up with an excuse to release Sandoval from custody. We knew El Zorro kept extensive records of his clients and his operation, but I couldn't convince Benito to execute a search warrant on his office.

Back at PGR headquarters in Piedras Negras, the casualness of how the case was being handled concerned me and my gut instinct told me to stay on top of these guys until the end. The intended illegal migrants milled freely around the entry foyer, although I felt confident they wouldn't flee and raise the ire of the Mexican Federales. El Zorro was placed in a holding cell along with his cohorts but they too didn't seem very concerned with what was going on. The passengers were debriefed in the open area and statements taken. Since they were still in Mexico and hadn't figured out we were American agents, they were very open as to where they were going in the United States and how much they were paying. The passports with photo substitutions were copied, but I couldn't get the Mexican agents to provide me a copy. Still, I was pleased none of the smugglers had been released. The incriminating statements pointed to an easy prosecution and, from what I could tell, another slam-dunk case like many of my cases before. But no action was being taken on El Zorro.

I was not going to be satisfied without a conviction. I had instructed the Eagle Pass agents to return to the United States, and I planned to have my staff from the consulate return to Monterrey as well.

"Mr. Acosta, it would be best if we stayed just to make sure they don't release El Zorro," FSN investigator Huerta told me.

He too had noticed their delay in filing charges against El Zorro. I made my decision. I would stay in their face along with Huerta until charges were filed. Throughout the rest of the day, through the night and the entire next day, one of us stayed inside the office right outside where El Zorro was being held. Our presence was much to the dismay of some of the agents tasked with drafting the documents for prosecution. The hours ticked by and no charging documents were produced. Instead the agents made excuses, horsing around and leaving the building for hours at a time. Benito was not around, and they made it clear they would not take direction from me. We were within hours of having to release El Zorro for lack of charges, and I was getting steamed, especially when one of the Mexican cops announced that they weren't going to be able to produce the necessary documentation in time. The attorneys had left for the evening and there was no one else qualified to draw up the forms.

"So sorry," the officer said with a smirk.

"If that's all that's holding us up, then there's no problem," I grinned. "My investigator is an attorney, so we will prepare the documents."

Before anyone could object, Huerta sat down at one of the desks and began writing up the charges. The officers were dumbfounded. They had run out of excuses and had no other ways to stop us from moving ahead with the prosecution.

El Zorro, meanwhile, was in a cell on the bottom floor of the building. He was smug and self-assured as he comforted his wife, who had come to visit. He told her he'd be free and on his way home soon. He was sorely mistaken. A few days later he was still in jail, charged with falsification of documents and Article 138, which dealt with illegal exportation of Mexican nationals to a foreign country. His five subordinates were all charged with being accessories.

The Mexican media gave great coverage when a press conference was held to announce the arrest of El Zorro. I need to emphasize that this was the *first* time a Mexican smuggler was arrested in Mexico transporting Mexicans to the border to introduce them into the United States illegally.

Initially we had been gearing up to place El Zorro in a U.S. prison for "crimes committed against the United States." However, after his guilty verdict, he was sentenced to thirteen years in a Mexican prison, much more time than he would have received in our country. Had he known, I feel certain that El Zorro would have preferred justice on the U.S. side.

A funny thing happened after the case was over. Our office in Mexico City asked its branch offices throughout the country to submit great examples of law enforcement cooperation between Mexico and United States. As I had told Villareal, Attorney General Janet Reno was visiting Mexico soon and she wanted to highlight some great cooperation stories. None of them submitted anything because, frankly, they didn't have any cases like that. The only one that was sent to her office was El Zorro's. Several months later I received a call from Benito Villareal. To my great surprise, he informed me that he had been contacted about the Reno visit by Antonio Lozano, the attorney general of Mexico. He wanted to know about the El Zorro prosecution because Janet Reno had supposedly thanked him personally for Mexico's cooperation. I was quite amused.

When I had told Villareal about Reno's interest, he had blown it off as bullcrap. He later told me he had wanted to tell me then that I was full of shit. Now he wanted to tell me that yes, he could see I really did have those high-level connections. Laughing, I told him I was merely a foot soldier like himself and glad of the opportunity we had to work together. When I transferred from Monterrey, I felt proud walking into his office to find a plaque of appreciation I had presented to him on his wall. It meant a lot. He was not aware I would be dropping by, so I knew he had not just hung it to impress me.

Recently I had the opportunity to visit with our FNS investigators in Monterrey, where I learned that El Zorro did his time, returned to Nueva Rosita, and is allegedly back to his old tricks. Maybe it's time to contact Benito Villareal and put him on the case again.

CHAPTER TEN

The Young and Innocent

EIGHTEEN-MONTH-OLD DIEGO JOSE Gomez sobbed uncontrollably amid the confusion at the detention center in Guatemala City, Guatemala, as immigration authorities separated more than fifty children from the smugglers transporting them to the United States. The seasoned officials were smitten by the cute, charismatic El Salvadoran boy traveling in blue polkadot pajamas, as if he were on a short drive with his parents. A few young female officers, most of them mothers themselves, wiped away tears as the terrified children scrambled to draw comfort from anybody they thought was safe. The young travelers had been entrusted to human smugglers with a subspecialty in transporting children to the United States. Their parents could only hope the smugglers would successfully deliver them safely across the border where they were waiting for them, several thousand miles away. The hope did not come cheaply. The fee for each child was more than five thousand dollars.

Half kidding, several of the immigration officers offered to adopt Little Diego, as he became known, along with his seven-year-old-brother Eduardo. Their five-year-old cousin was also traveling with them. Diego and Eduardo's parents had left El Salvador for the United States three months earlier in search of a better life and had settled in Washington, D.C. They had no problem finding employment there, and after saving up their money for the smuggling fees, they had sent for the two little boys, who had been left behind with their maternal grandparents in El Salvador.

Eduardo didn't realize the delay had nothing to do with money. "My mama paid so they could take us," Eduardo stated confidently. He was a self-assured little man as he tried to console his little brother.

"Don't worry, Diego," he calmly told him. "Mama will be coming for us." His confidence in itself was heartbreaking.

A little girl, seven-year-old Brenda, was talking to another of our officers. "Three years ago, my mommy left for the United States," she told him. "That's why I don't remember her face very well, but now I will be going to see her so that I will know her."

For Diego, Eduardo, their cousin, and Brenda, the journey had come to an end. They would not be seeing their parents anytime soon. Thankfully Diego and his travel buddies had not gotten very far on their odyssey. They were only a hundred miles from San Salvador, so their grandparents arrived to pick them up within a day or two. The grandparents almost seemed relieved and happy that the children's ordeal had stopped before going further. There were tears of joy when they collected them in their arms. They had not been comfortable when the three little boys left El Salvador with complete strangers, and had wondered if they would see them again.

Our intervention had prevented this group of fifty-three from suffering hunger, unforgiving weather, abuse, or worse. Maybe we had even derailed a life in slavery or prostitution—stories of children being sold to human traffickers along the way were not uncommon. Our tightened border patrols, especially after 9/11, was making it more difficult and expensive to cross into the United States. It was also making it harder for those already in the United States illegally to return home to retrieve their children, forcing them to hire coyotes. They couldn't afford to round-trip it themselves, plus pay the fee for a child or two. Often they could only afford to bring one family member at a time. Usually the wife was the first to cross, and when enough money was saved up, the children would follow, sometimes together, sometimes not.

In my first undercover operation in the back of the U-Haul from Juarez to Chicago, Pedro Marquez's wife and six children had been with me. Pedro had paid three thousand eight hundred and fifty dollars to the Medina family to ship them together. Señora Marquez had protected her children throughout the journey, never letting anyone be separated from her. It would have been unthinkable to have any of her children travel alone.

The post-9/11 world saw a spike in child-smuggling rings. Parents were given the impression that their children would be well cared for, and the journeys would be easy. Coyotes were known to abandon the children they were transporting if they thought anyone was on to them. They would also deprive the children of food and water to reduce their need to go to the bathroom. There were also reports of physical and sexual abuse. Some children died during their journey.

As recently as April 2011, I read about an eight-year-old girl from El Salvador whose parents had entrusted her to smugglers to get her to Los Angeles, where they lived. Along the way, she was raped not only by the smugglers, but by a seventeen-year-old fellow passenger as well. The men poked her with a needle to get her to open her legs.

Back at the detention center in Guatemala City, the authorities were trying to process all the children. Their main objective was to repatriate the victims with their source families, and their identification was not necessarily helpful. The task was monumental, consular and immigration issues being only a part of the problem. Some of the children were so young they weren't sure themselves how they had gotten as far as they had. The lucky ones were reclaimed by their relatives, sooner rather than later.

The detention center was squalid. It was filled to capacity with immigrants from around the world who had been intercepted while trying to get into Mexico. They were from Central and South America, as well as the Middle East and Asia. The center was overcrowded and lacked sufficient sanitary facilities. It was a windowless, prisonlike sprawl. Women and children were kept separately from the men, in a very rudimentary attempt to enhance everyone's safety.

This group of fifty children that included Diego and Eduardo had originated in San Salvador, where twelve coyotes had put them on a bus. Normally they wouldn't travel in such a large group, but because of a backlog in the pipeline the coyotes decided to move them all at once.

We had learned about the child smuggling ring from two outstanding INS agents assigned to our office in El Salvador, Eddie Sotomayor and Abraham Lugo. Their investigation revealed that Berta Campos, an El Salvadoran woman with two prior deportations from the United States, and several others, had been running the lucrative criminal enterprise that had smuggled hundreds to the United States over an eight-year period.

Campos charged between four and five thousand dollars to the children's parents, who were living in the United States illegally and had a very difficult time scraping together the funds. They took a leap of faith that the children would be safe with the smugglers, because other options were almost impossible.

Maintaining surveillance on this group, our agents observed the coyotes loading the fifty children onto a bus that eventually departed San Salvador for Guatemala. Since the bus was still in-country, there were no violations and our officers had to wait until the bus entered Guatemalan territory to detain the group.

"We will track and we will find Berta Rosa Campos. There is no place that she can hide where we can't get her and we will prosecute her ass along with her top lieutenants," I told my agents. Campos was the ringleader of the smuggling operation, moving the underage immigrants from El Salvador to Los Angeles, Washington, D.C., and New York City. According to several sources, numerous children had been lost or abandoned along the way and never made it to their final destination.

Our investigation had begun a few months earlier when we received information that four children were being kept in an open backyard of a drop house in Mexico City. Working closely with officials from the Mexican Federal Preventive Police, we located them and discovered they had been staying outdoors even at night when the temperatures dipped to nearly freezing. They had not eaten for three days. We soon learned that two others had been abandoned by the smugglers and put out in the streets of Tijuana. By sheer luck, we were able to find two kids, both under the age of ten, wandering around town. It was time to put Campos and her smuggling band out of business.

Throughout the many undercover smuggling operations I worked on, I had personally seen the ordeals, the suffering, and the resilience of immigrants adamant about reaching our country, a great number of them to reunite with family members already here. Adults might be subservient to the smugglers because of their fear, but at least they could understand why certain things were happening and could take some responsibility for the predicament. For children, however, not only were they not capable of defending themselves, but they had no idea how they had come into harm's way. Little ones like Diego, his brother, and his cousin were relying on the scavengers of society to keep them safe. Seventeen of the children in this group were under the age of ten, and the oldest of the bunch was seventeen. They were a valuable load. This group alone would have brought in almost a quarter of a million dollars, half of which had already been paid.

When I was a young agent on undercover missions, I had assumed responsibility for lots of children—the sixteen-year-old smuggled with me in the trunk of a small car in Southern California and the two kids who rode in the back of the U-Haul with me, to name just a few introduced in these pages. Keeping my eye on these children was not in my job description, but it was a responsibility I took very seriously.

Central Americans, Asians, South Americans, and just about every nationality traverse the long distance from Guatemala to the southern U.S. border by train, bus, private vehicles, and, often, in the back of tractor trailers. It took over twenty-four hours to make the 650-mile trip between Guatemala and Mexico City, and that was barely halfway to the U.S. border.

The large amount of money parents in the United States pay to the smugglers gives them hope their children will be treated humanely, will not be subject to abuse, and will arrive safely in their homes. Unfortunately, this is often not the case.

I learned that U.S. Immigration and Customs Enforcement in Phoenix had rescued three children from El Salvador who were being held by smugglers. Their parents had paid them $13,000. Once in Phoenix, the smugglers demanded an additional $6,500. When this was paid, they demanded another $7,000. At that point, the parents decided to contact authorities. The ensuing investigation led to the rescue of the children but none of the smugglers was arrested.

In another instance, Arizona Department of Public Safety officers had stopped a tractor trailer a few miles north of the border town of Nogales, Arizona, and discovered ninety-seven immigrants being smuggled in the back of the trailer, including fourteen children and two pregnant women. The refrigerated trailer was loaded with seventeen pallets of mangos and chilled to 34 degrees. The immigrants had already paid $3,000 each for smuggling fees to the northern Mexican border and another $3,000 for the next leg of their journey to Phoenix, hardly the ideal way to travel for the price they paid.

I was adamant that we would make sure we brought Berta Campos and her cohorts to face U.S. justice. I didn't believe in just arresting drivers of loads and coyotes. I believed in going after the masterminds behind these crimes. Unfortunately this sentiment was not shared by all in my agency, especially at our headquarters in Washington, D.C. I suggested that we "parole" several children into the United States to reunite them with their parents, so we could use them as witnesses to obtain warrants. But I was told no. That was not the answer I wanted, so I took my idea to Warren Lewis, the district director of our office in D.C. Warren was a good friend and the father of my godson, Aaron.

"I need your help with the U.S. attorney's office to prosecute Berta Campos and I need it quick," I told him.

I explained that Guatemalan authorities were holding a number of Campos's smugglers. I had assigned officers to watch the perimeter of the detention center in Guatemala City so they couldn't bribe their way out of custody. Roy Hernandez, our acting officer in charge in Guatemala, and I had contacted the Guatemalan immigration director and received his assurance that if we obtained warrants for the smugglers, they would be expelled to the United States to face charges here.

Warren and I had developed a great relationship with the U.S. attorney's office in Washington, D.C. We had been so successful in prosecuting cases through their office that we usually had no problem having them accepted for prosecution. But this time we were asking for something out of the ordinary: child witnesses allowed into the country to testify against their smugglers. It was going to be quite a bureaucratic ordeal to get them in; we would have to track down the parents of any child we allowed in and convince them to sign a consent form to allow their child to testify for the government. In exchange for their testimony, the children would be permitted to join and stay with their parents in the United States while the investigation was ongoing and during the subsequent prosecution.

The problem was, many of the children couldn't provide us with the contact information for their parents, so Lugo and Sotomayor immediately set out to convince relatives in El Salvador to provide it to us. They were good at what they did and soon had a listing of several parents in the States. When contact was made and the parents expressed a reluctance to cooperate, I started calling them personally. I told them horror stories about what had happened to children we had rescued in Mexico City and Tijuana, who had traveled with the same smugglers. After that they agreed, although many of them assumed we were setting a trap and that they were going to be deported along with their children. But they were horrified enough by my accounts to be willing to take the risk.

Through interviewing the children and the parents we determined who the main smugglers were in the group. Warrants were obtained on Ana Karina Cruz Rivas, Juan Orlando Servellon De Leon, Andrea Giron, Guillermo Antonio Paniaqua, and the ringleader, Berta Campos. Sotomayor and

Lugo were able to have authorities from El Salvador arrest seven other members of the ring including Berta Campos's son and former daughter-in-law and charge them with smuggling violations.

Campos went into hiding in Guatemala. Fearing that officials in that country would detain her, she somehow made her way to Los Angeles. Seven of the twelve smugglers detained with the children on the bus in Guatemala were charged in El Salvador. Indictments were returned in Washington, D.C., on the five others, Berta Campos and four El Salvadorans. The four were expelled from Guatemala and arrested upon their arrival in Houston. We captured Campos in Los Angeles.

Journals confiscated in the investigation indicated that the ring had been operating since 1994 and smuggled hundreds of children into the United States. Every week, between ten and fifteen children were brought from their native countries, through Mexico and on to Los Angeles, where they were met by relatives or sent on to other destinations inside the United States. The trip typically took between ten and thirty days, and, depending on which smugglers were used, could include treks through deserts and isolated mountain passes. In many cases the children were held in deplorable conditions at drop houses throughout Mexico.

In 1995, Campos was deported for trying to smuggle two children into California. Three years later she was caught again trying to make it into the United States and was sent back. She employed her husband, two sons, her two daughters, and her daughter-in-law in her business. An informant alleged that some of the children might have suffered sexual abuse during the trips, and that pornographic videos may have been made. A thirteen-year-old girl told authorities that a smuggler from the ring warned her about two men who were bringing her to Tijuana. She said he told her that they liked touching little girls. These allegations were never substantiated.

Campos had been traveling in and out of the United States without difficulty, flying directly into Los Angeles. Normally the organization only transported ten to fifteen children per week but because their groups had been backed up, Campos had decided they would clear the backlog in one large load. This had been their demise, but we still had big Berta to track down.

Our agents in El Salvador determined that she made it into Los Angeles and that several children were being held at the house where she was staying. We immediately sent word to our Los Angeles office. Dismally, the officers took too long to respond and by the time they went, she was gone. Even worse, they found a small number of children who didn't belong to the occupants of the house, but the officers decided to leave them there because they didn't have car seats to transport them. I was livid and called the head of the Los Angeles office. By the time they returned, there was nobody there.

We would take no more chances, so I dispatched Special Agent Carlos Archuleta to Los Angeles to find Berta Campos. Archuleta had been stationed in Los Angeles and still had quite a number of contacts in the area. Within a few days he established where she was hiding and what identity she was using. The time had come for her to face justice, even if she had not been caught with a single immigrant present.

Berta Rosa Campos and four other smugglers were sent to Washington, D.C., to stand trial on charges of conspiracy to commit immigrant smuggling. They all pled guilty to the charges but unfortunately, in exchange for not going to trial, served only a short period of time before they were deported back to their countries of origin.

Not long after Berta's arrest, I joined District Director Lewis in Washington, D.C., and top INS officials for a press conference to announce the breakup of this child smuggling syndicate, which was at that time the largest in the history of our agency.

For all the young ones who had been exploited, hurt, and abandoned along the way, I hoped that a measure of justice had been served. For those parents in the United States illegally, I hoped our message to keep their children in their homeland, rather than place them in an extremely high-risk situation with scoundrels, rapists, and murderers, who prefer the term *transporters,* would hit home. Sadly, my audience wasn't large enough.

CHAPTER ELEVEN

Operation Montoneros

"How do I know you guys are not FBI agents? Those guys have been after me for a long time?" asked Gladys Perdomo Board in perfect English as Agent Arthur Nieto and I settled into a booth with her at Yuppy's. It was a trendy, popular bar in the tourist section La Zona Rosa, in the heart of Mexico City.

"Gladys, the FBI wouldn't have the balls to be here in Mexico City. Besides, they can only work in the U.S.," I replied as I looked across the street and spotted the two FSN investigators I had assigned as lookouts to make sure we weren't being followed. I noticed that the investigator I stationed outside had not taken off his sunglasses, the signal he was to give me if he spotted anything out of the ordinary. I already had one encounter with the Mexican Federal Judicial Police (MFJP) in Monterrey while working on this case and had been able to get out without being hurt. Our source, who himself had been working for the MFJP at the checkpoint near Reynosa, told us that Gladys not only paid to have her "Other Than Mexican" immigrants go through but also used the federal agents to provide protection and "dirty" work if needed. I had worked many undercover cases on the northern Mexican border, but this was different. I was more than one thousand miles away from our border and without a weapon.

After a couple of drinks, Gladys was soon yakking away, bragging about her immigrant smuggling operation, how she had federal policemen working for her and how much money she was making. Gladys, who was in her early fifies, still retained some of her beautiful features, but her time on the run and the pressures of running an international immigrant smuggling operation had taken their toll. I did not lie to her. We were not FBI agents, we were U.S. immigration agents.

When the average person thinks of a smuggler, they usually think of a smarmy, immoral, thieving male scumbag. When the name Gladys Perdomo Board came across my desk, I was intrigued. I had never hunted down a female smuggler, or one with such an established international reputation. In fact, her enterprise covered more territory than any male smuggler I had ever encountered.

Gladys's name was dropped on us by a *madrina*, a hench-man for some corrupted MFJP officers. He had walked into our office out of the blue. Knowing the dire consequences they might encounter, *madrinas*, or godmothers, were not known for ratting out their bosses. They aspired to be federal police themselves, though undoubtedly shady ones, and were willing to do just about anything to impress their controlling MFJP officer. They did the dirty work, including collecting bribes and roughing up people on demand.

The *madrina* who paid us a visit in Monterrey asked to speak to someone about an immigrant smuggling organization specializing in Middle Eastern and Chinese immigrants. He was upset about being cut out of the profits by both his regular MFJP handlers and a smuggler named Gladys Perdomo Board. He said she had stiffed him on a two-thousand-dollar bribe, and he was turning her in.

Gladys was fifty-one when she first appeared on our radar. By then she was operating her own profitable franchise of a well-organized international smuggling ring. The organization transported high-paying clients who forked over twenty-eight thousand dollars each for the journey from point of origin to the United States. About fifty immigrants a month came through Gladys's part of the pipeline. They originated in China, Pakistan, and India and went first to Cuba or to Nicaragua, then to Guatemala, where they would cross by land into southern Mexico. From there they were transported to northern Mexico, passing through Gladys's territory, where she would be paid per head.

Gladys did not fit the stereotype of an immigrant smuggler. She was college-educated, didn't grow up in poverty, was a successful businesswoman, and had become a naturalized U.S. citizen. She was born in 1944 in La Ceiba, a port city on the northern coast of Honduras. Her father was a top administrator in the Department of Elections, and her uncle had served as head of customs and head of ports. Gladys attended the

Instituto Maria Regina, a private, all-girls Catholic college supposedly funded by the Standard Fruit Company, the first American company to operate in Mexico and one of the country's biggest employers. Gladys earned a degree in education, although she never worked as a teacher. She found a job with the Elections Commission in La Ceiba. When she was in her early thirties, she traveled to the United States, where she met and married James Board, an engineer who lived in Houston. The marriage enabled her to become a U.S. citizen. The couple had three children, but they later divorced.

Gladys needed to become gainfully employed, so she earned her real estate license and found a job at a local real estate agency before starting one of her own. Some of her clients were shady characters involved in drug trafficking, and she soon found herself pressured by the DEA and FBI into giving them information. According to Gladys, a federal agent had threatened her with arrest and twenty years in prison if she didn't cooperate. If this is true, the agent was lying to her, but for someone born and raised in Latin America, such a threat would be taken seriously, so she started helping them with information on dealers they assigned to her. Later, when I got to know Gladys, I came to the conclusion she got a thrill from these investigations. Unfortunately, the agents did not conceal her identity and she felt that she and her family were in danger. Believing a warrant for her arrest would be issued, she stopped snitching and fled south of the border.

In Guatemala, she went to work for a smuggling ring with a reputation for taking care of its clients. Its market was Central Americans who wanted to cross through Mexico into the United States. The money she could make smuggling far outweighed the small risk she would be arrested. In her livelihood, smugglers with a good reputation among clients were not considered reprobates, but rather respected business operators who were doing a noble service for the disenfranchised.

Markets for smugglers were on the rise throughout Latin America. The number of U.S.-bound illegal immigrants coming from the Far East and Eastern Europe had increased substantially after eastern bloc countries made it easier to get exit visas. Coupled with our tightening of legal requirements for immigration, business for opportunistic smugglers in this part of the world was booming.

Many smugglers had been taking advantage of sea routes and lax U.S. Coast Guard surveillance to move immigrants by sea, until the mishap of a poor excuse for a ship, the *Golden Venture*. It became stranded off Rockaway Beach, Queens, within sight of New York City in the spring of 1993. To get that far, the passengers on board had crossed the mountains between China and Thailand on foot, boarded a small transport boat in Bangkok, sailed to Mombasa, Kenya, where they changed vessels and picked up more passengers, then circled the Cape of Good Hope en route to the United States. The two-year, seventeen-thousand-mile odyssey ended on June 6 when the rusted hulk of a ship ran aground after a mutiny on board. The 286 illegal Chinese immigrants and thirteen crew members jumped into the frigid water in an attempt to swim to shore. Ten people drowned. The rest were rescued and detained by U.S. immigration officials. After that incident, maritime intervention along both the Atlantic and Pacific coasts was intensified, making it much harder to reach the United States by sea.

In Latin America, many smuggling rings operated only certain legs of the whole journey. Some moved immigrants from points of origin into the Caribbean or Central America, where others would pick up the route into the United States. Such was the case with Gladys. Her trek into the United States was the final arc of a worldwide smuggling route.

After the *madrina*'s initial information on Gladys, we learned from an informant that she was housing some Indian and Pakistani immigrants in a dusty Mexican town about sixty miles northeast of Monterrey. I soon found myself in that desolate place, the town of China, in Nuevo León, watching the safe house that had been identified by our guy, and I spotted several individuals walking outside that fit the description.

Next, a Honduran man we had arrested carrying one of her loads gave me a telephone introduction to her in exchange for leniency. Gladys was extremely shrewd, so she was suspicious of the call, knowing her driver was in jail and had likely provided authorities with her contact information in a deal. She was cordial but she gave me no openings.

Then my informant and I did surveillance on the Virrey Hotel, her base of operation in Reynosa. The hotel also served as an unofficial headquarters for MFJP officers assigned temporarily to the area, some of whom were on Gladys's payroll. MFJP had a reputation for having some of the most corrupt law enforcement officers in the world. We heard rumors that anyone wanting to serve with them had to "buy" their positions and continue paying up the chain at each level of promotion. Top positions along the northern Mexican border were said to "sell" for up to half a million dollars. Corrupt federal judicial police profited from every kind of criminal activity, including immigrant smuggling.

Across Mexico, MFJP officers frequently operate from rented hotel rooms when assigned away from their home areas. I was watching the hotel from a parking lot across the street when a group of men in uniform surrounded my car. MFJP officers had intercepted the calls I was making from my cellular phone to Special Agent Noe Dominguez in McAllen, Texas, which sits across the border from Reynosa. One of Gladys's groups was scheduled to be smuggled into the United States that night, and I intended to follow them to the river, pinpoint their location, and have the transporters arrested. This would provide me with an opening to slide in as one of her drivers.

I was startled when they surrounded my vehicle in Reynosa, two of them pointing their guns at me from the front of my vehicle. "Holy shit, here I go again," was the only thing that I could think of at the time.

The MFJP thug who pulled me out and slammed me onto my vehicle must have weighed around 225 pounds. He was a strong son of a bitch. My weapon was inside my vehicle but I knew it would be useless to me even if I'd had it within reach. My cell phone, on the other hand, was my lifeline and I had to prevent them from taking it.

"I am a fucking American with diplomatic immunity!" I yelled at one of the guys who seemed to be in charge. When he asked if I had a weapon, I told them where it was. My status threw a monkey wrench into their plans and it took a few minutes before they told me they were taking me in. I replied I had no problem but asked they take the handcuffs off.

Once they were off, one of their agents was assigned to drive my vehicle. I insisted on riding with him and while en route, I speed-dialed the U.S. Embassy and got through to Agent Arthur Nieto and briefed him on what had happened. The MFJP officer was pissed but there was nothing he could do. His boss would not be a happy camper when we got to their detention facility. Just like my first encounter with Mexican cops, getting a phone call through by sheer luck had saved the day for me. Although the arrest had rattled me, I only lay low for a couple of days before resuming my surveillance.

It would take several more calls with Gladys before she finally agreed to meet me at a popular bar in Mexico City. She was a master smuggler, bold and unafraid in her role as the boss. She meted out orders to corrupt Mexican cops and her criminal subordinates with the same hard-ass authority as her male counterparts.

Sitting in Yuppy's talking and drinking, Gladys became loquacious and personal. She confided in me that she was in an abusive relationship with a younger smuggler, and he and his family were always taking advantage of her, milking her for money and manhandling her.

To be honest, hearing about this smuggler's love life was the last thing I thought I'd ever be doing. I wasn't even supposed to be working this case. Being a senior official at the U.S. consulate and an administrator, I had merely wanted to pass the information about Gladys to agents with the McAllen Border Patrol's Anti-Smuggling Unit or the Investigations Branch of the Houston District Office and let them take charge. But neither office was interested in this complex, transnational case, so I had gone undercover myself.

Gladys was short, well-built, and sophisticated. Her deeply tanned face was creased, and strands of gray streaked her brown, shoulder-length hair. I paid attention to her as if she were the only woman in the place, and smiled broadly as she recounted her stories and victories, and detailed her plans for the future.

"Gladys, you are amazing," I told her. "I have never met a woman with so much guts and smarts in this business."

She was a great talker. I think it had been many years since she had received this type of flirtatious attention. Every once in a while, I'd laugh loudly at one of her stories, reach over, and softly touch her hand and say, "I like listening to you." I needed to string this smuggling queen along so she would agree to meet me again, and by the end of the evening she thought that I was her new best friend.

The next time I met Gladys, I brought along David Ramirez, an undercover agent from the Houston office. As luck would have it, Gladys also came with a friend, Marisol Camacho, who took a liking to Ramirez.

Marisol's family was part of a loosely grouped association of families that served as clearinghouses just south of Mexico City. They did not make tons of money, but several hundred people arrived and departed from their properties on a daily basis. Families like the Camachos are found throughout the entire smuggling route. They might be considered low-level smugglers, but their participation is crucial. Because they make less than the top smugglers, they are also prone to abuse the illegal migrants who they feel are beneath them. When I learned of this clearinghouse, I traveled to the location and was astounded to see what was going on. Near a PEMEX gas station, dozens of little shacks covered the desolate and dusty area. Spending most of the day on foot so as not to attract attention, I watched two tractor trailers arrive during dusk and each unload well over one hundred poor souls. The people were herded into numerous adobe shacks, where they were to be separated depending on their destination. Some were going to Brownsville, others to Laredo, and yet others were destined for Baja, California. These people had endured twenty hours in the back of overheated tractor trailers and were not even halfway to the border. There were children, women, and elderly travelers. There seemed to be no demographic not represented. I saw Chinese, Pakistanis, Indians, and other nationalities in the groups.

The shacks themselves were deplorable and depressing. I managed to peek inside one and saw the large group of people inside sitting on the floor, leaning back against the wall for support.

The Camachos operated both a drop house and the small store where the people purchased their groceries. They marked up prices with abandon, knowing that the migrants had no other options.

Marisol wasn't traveling with Gladys on business, being a much lower-level operator, but she was seeking excitement, and tonight her presence worked well to fill out the foursome. A few more drinks and Gladys agreed to hire me as a driver.

Over the next several weeks, Ramirez and I transported several small groups of Chinese, Pakistani, Salvadoran, Indian, and Colombian nationals to Houston. Once, I drove a group of Pakistani and Indian immigrants who nearly starved to death. I had laid in near the drop house where they were keeping them in China, Nuevo León, about two hours south of the border. For a whole day I had observed them in the backyard, unattended by anyone. Those poor guys must be hungry, I thought to myself. They were leaving late that evening, so I met with Domingo, the river guide and operator of the stash house near the river.

"Domingo, here's a hundred dollars. Get some food for the group tonight and make sure they eat well before you take them into McAllen," I told him. I went back to the U.S. side to wait for them.

We were scheduled to leave early the next morning so I rented a room in McAllen not far from the hotel where the immigrants were to be taken that night. When Domingo called and said he was already with the group at the hotel, I decided to try to get some rest. Sleep was hard to come by with so many details to be worked out for the following day. I decided to pay our clients a visit and make sure they were staying quiet. Domingo was not in the room with the group like he was supposed to be. As I opened the door, I noticed that some meat on a couple of paper plates had not been touched.

"Hey, did you guys eat already?" I asked one of the young guys in the group.

"No sir, we do not eat meat and we are very, very hungry. We have not eaten much for two days," he responded.

That scumbag, I thought to myself. He had purposely served them pork, knowing full well they couldn't eat it. This way he could buy very little meat and could make more money for himself. I was disgusted and appalled, but I would deal with him later when it came time to pay him his part. Undercover or not, I have always honored the beliefs and traditions of all people, from wherever they hailed and however they came to be where they were. To have such disrespect for a fellow human being upset me to the core.

"Come on, you and I are going to get some food for you guys," I told the young guy. I scared the shit out of him, since Domingo had led them to believe that he was the main man, and they didn't want to piss him off.

"No sir, we are fine," he said. I told him it was okay and that he wouldn't have to worry about Domingo. I didn't have to push too much before the desire for food won out over fear.

I took one of the men to an H-E-B grocery store to purchase fruit and vegetables for his group. I thought he was going to faint at the quantities and selections of food. I got joy just from watching him load up his shopping cart with lots of fresh produce and edibles acceptable to his religion.

Over time, Gladys accepted me in her inner circle and felt comfortable enough to share information about her international smuggling activities. She said her main contact and mover in Central America was a man named Carlos Sanchez. Sanchez was an articulate, intelligent accountant who became involved with immigrant smuggling in his twenties. He knew almost every bigwig involved in the business throughout the region, being a dual citizen of Mexico and El Salvador.

Gladys's other important contact was Navtej Pall Singh Sandhu, a British citizen of Indian ancestry. Because of lax immigration visa requirements and rampant corruption, Indian and Pakistani immigrants had no difficulty entering Ecuador. A large community of migrants from these countries had accumulated over a period of time, as they waited for funds from their U.S. relatives to continue with their northward travels.

Sandhu had joined forces with Sanchez and Gladys, solidifying her leg of the route, moving Indian, Pakistani, and Middle Eastern immigrants to the United States. Sandhu had long been involved in smuggling, but he stayed in Ecuador, even though his operation was based in Nicaragua, where he had a great number of Nicaraguan officials on his payroll. This way he was able to receive immigrants coming from Peru, Ecuador or directly from Cuba and hold them in his stash house without being busted.

The majority of the clients were Indian and were coming to the United States as underpaid labor in Indian restaurants or fast-food chains.

Gladys moved them in loads from the Guatemalan border all the way to the U.S. border, almost 1,300 miles. There other smugglers would take them across. Gladys operated her safe houses in Mexico City, the journey's halfway point, as well as in the border town of Reynosa. She brazenly used public buses to take them to the border.

Moving undocumented immigrants past internal checkpoints required bribes, and Gladys said she always started at the top. She told us she never bothered with the little guys, only the really important officials. Niranjan Mann Singh was probably her most prominent associate. He was one of the ringleaders of the international smuggling enterprise that Gladys subcontracted with, at the time the largest operation in the world. Singh was flying illegal immigrants, mostly Indians, from Russia to Cuba to Ecuador. Gladys said she had traveled to Panama to negotiate with Singh and Panamanian officials to have Middle Easterners staged there for transport north.

We knew that Gladys ran an extremely well-organized

business. Unfortunately, capturing her was complicated by the protection she received from corrupt government and law enforcement officials in the countries where she based her operations.

During my meetings with Gladys, she made it clear that she was interested in a romantic liaison with me, and her friend Marisol had taken a liking to Ramirez. We'd flirt just enough to be believable. But Gladys was getting frustrated. One time, when I arrived at her hotel to pick up some money, she answered the door wrapped seductively in a towel. I fumbled through some excuse why I couldn't stay, something about providing meals for the people at the drop house. I said I'd be back in a couple of hours. When I failed to return, she was beyond annoyed. The next morning I told her that I had gotten drunk and fallen asleep, and I begged to be forgiven.

The evening of the arrest, we promised Gladys and Marisol that tonight was the night, once all the immigrants in the group we were currently transporting were smuggled into the United States. We said the "fun" would occur at the Holiday Inn in McAllen. In gleeful anticipation, Gladys, a U.S. citizen, crossed through the McAllen port of entry with me and proceeded to the hotel. Marisol had no documents, so she was going to cross the river with the immigrants.

When we got the call that the group was on its way, Ramirez took off for the border to meet them. Marisol, all decked out and ready to party, approached him to give him a hug. He quickly placed her in handcuffs. Once we got word that Marisol and the others were in custody, Agent Noe Dominguez, my partner, and I proceeded to the hotel to arrest Gladys. She had already ordered two drinks for her and me and was anxiously waiting to get on the dance floor to boogie. I gave Dominguez the signal, he identified himself as a federal agent, and she was informed that she was under arrest.

She was shocked at the turn of events and looked wistfully to me, thinking I could save her. I took out my badge and credentials, further devastating her. It didn't take long, though, for Gladys to be her feisty self again, offering to assist in any way she could if we would reduce the charges.

Gladys offered to help us get an arrest on a crooked MFJP by the name of Gabriel Velazquez, who was on her payroll. She was going to lure the scoundrel over the border by telling him she wanted to give him his share of the smuggling gains, but she needed to meet him on the U.S. side because she would be leaving for Houston in a few short hours. Velazquez agreed to meet her in a guest room at the McAllen Best Western hotel later that morning.

I contacted the supervisor of the McAllen Sector with the information. He agreed to meet me there with a team of agents for the takedown. One hour before Gladys was to rendezvous with Velazquez, I arrived at the hotel, but nobody from McAllen was there. Concerned, I called headquarters to find out what was going on.

To my surprise, the supervisor who answered the phone told me to come in about the impending arrest. I found it strange, but thought perhaps he had new information. I hurried to headquarters, where I was informed that they would not be participating in Velazquez's arrest after all. The deputy chief had also made it clear that the criminal cop was not to be taken into custody in their sector. I couldn't believe it. I was unable to contact the deputy chief directly, and Velazquez would be arriving at the hotel shortly, so I decided my only option was to arrest him myself. I hurried to the Best Western but I was too late. Velasquez had already arrived, smelled a trap after asking the receptionist some questions, and hurried off.

Gladys was not discouraged. She reached the rat by phone, but he said he was about to go on duty and would not return to McAllen that day. We knew we had missed our one and only chance. The thug was eventually indicted, but that was the best we could do.

From the start, the deputy chief of the McAllen Sector had not been a supporter of our investigation. The man didn't even seem to be particularly impressed that we had taken down a huge smuggling operation. I guess having it done by an agent who was not on his staff humiliated him. It was evidence that his own program was not very effective. I had worked my butt off during the investigation. I was the person who had started the case, done the undercover work, directed the other agents, and written the report. I presented it, practically tied with a bow, to one of the McAllen agents for his signature, still basically giving the sector credit for the takedown. However, there was no way our foreign district was going to be denied the credit it deserved.

The jockeying for position over the press conference to announce the arrests was embarrassing. I wrote the initial press release and was given permission by our district director in Mexico City to represent that district. However, the deputy chief in McAllen ordered it rewritten and rescheduled the media event. Finally, the internal squabbling and scratching ended. I purchased a new shirt at a local mall and headed to the station. Numerous vans filled with news crews were descending on the scene. At five minutes till two, I walked into the press room to announce the grand success of the operation.

With the cameras rolling, Chief Patrol Agent Joe Garza from McAllen walked in and thanked me for the case and for joining him in the announcement. He seemed genuine in his praise, and I sincerely doubted he was aware of the backstage bullshit that had gone down before our shaking hands at the podium. Not knowing too much about the case, he read from prepared remarks and turned the press conference over to me.

I was undeniably proud of this case, which we called Operation Montoneros. I had never known a federal agent to do the undercover work, write the reports, coordinate the surveillance, secure the warrants of arrests, and finish up the case by holding a press conference to announce the results of the criminal investigation.

Despite the sector's unwillingness to assist me with the investigation, I was appreciative of the guys who had provided backup, especially my assistant officer in charge, Alfonso Pineda. The operation was a great credit to our agency. When I later learned from Doris Meissner, commissioner of the INS, that she had never been briefed and had known nothing about Operation Montoneros, I was flabbergasted, but I refused to get sucked back into the office politics. I chose to stay focused on the mission's success.

Gladys Perdomo Board agreed to plead guilty to a single charge of conspiracy. Six other counts of illegal immigrant smuggling against her were then dropped. In her plea, she described how she moved fifty South Asian immigrants a month into the United States over the Texas border. She said she made approximately eight thousand dollars per person, enabling her to live a lavish lifestyle. She told us about her two residences, a $400,000 home in Houston and a smaller vacation home in Mexico, and her fancy, fully loaded Mercedes-Benz. Gladys let us know she took very good care of her clients, better by far than most smugglers. She said the proof was that she wouldn't get paid if they didn't arrive safely, so that alone guaranteed their humane treatment. Plus, she said, she had compassion for her clients. I found that hard to believe. I remembered her telling me that two years earlier there had been a catastrophic accident in which nineteen Hondurans had drowned after one of her boats had capsized in the Gulf of Mexico on its way north. She later denied the accident had ever happened, although during an appearance on ABC's *Nightline* with Ted Koppel, she recounted the event, describing how she went out each day looking at the sea hoping the immigrants would show up safely.

Instead of twenty years in prison, Gladys received a sentence of eighteen months in exchange for her cooperation with our government. The U.S. federal district judge who presided over her case was very critical of our operation, however. He felt compelled to criticize it on three levels: the amount of money we had spent on the operation, the minimal involvement of some of the defendants, and our tactics. As an example, he pointed to how Ramirez and I had faked a romantic interest in Gladys and Marisol to lure them across the border.

I heartily disagreed. The resources we dedicated to this case were minimal, yet the results had been astounding. We had shut down the entire operation headed by Gladys. The role and involvement of each of the defendants were indisputable, regardless of how important they were in Gladys's organization. Our undercover simulated roles played out in real life. We never crossed the line with our undercover disguises or tactics. The convictions of these criminal dirtbags bore that out. I had put international smugglers on notice that they were not going to operate with impunity outside our borders. It was my belief that we needed to aggressively go after the criminal smugglers outside the United States in order to stop them. Many of them believed that only if they crossed into the United States would they be prosecuted, so they usually left the job of crossing to underlings. This mistaken sense of security was shaken as a result of our bust.

In fact, throughout Operation Montoneros, I recorded many of my conversations with Gladys where she referred to other people in her ring. With this list of names, I soon headed the largest international manhunt the INS had ever known. Code-named Operation Seek & Keep, it would take me country-hopping undercover to net the big fish in charge of a sophisticated multinational smuggling operation like we had never seen.

Epilogue

THE IMMIGRATION ISSUE is as sensitive and polarizing today as it has ever been. The Immigration Reform and Control Act of 1986 resulted in the legalization of several million immigrants and the mistaken notion that a buildup of Border Patrol resources along our frontier would stop illegal immigration. The additional resources were needed, but this was just one piece of the solution. There are now ten to fifteen million illegal immigrants in the U.S. and that number continues to rise daily.

Finding work in the United States is the magnet that draws individuals here. Companies have been known to hire several thousand illegal immigrants. Conservatives and liberal politicians alike have all been recipients of financial support from these companies; in the meantime, each side blames the other about illegal immigration without doing anything about it.

The lack of interior enforcement has resulted in brazen

attitudes by illegal immigrants. Where once illegal immigrants feared and hid from immigration authorities, it is now common to see large numbers of them publicly protesting and demanding immigration reform. In some cases, these public displays have included raising the Mexican flag or desecrating the American flag.

Throughout my career, there was never a lack of information about *who* the major employment violators were. Businesses in the meat industry, landscaping, hotels and restaurants, just to name a few, have been major violators of immigration hiring laws. They are willing to hire undocumented workers because of the billions of dollars in profits they stand to reap. Only by curbing the opportunities for undocumented workers to find employment in the United States can we curb the flow of illegal immigrants.

Through my undercover operations, I joined many of these new pioneers in their travels, heard their stories, and saw firsthand the risks they experienced. I met good ones and I met bad ones. I came to know and arrest the drivers, drop-house keepers, and coyotes who moved the *pollos* across the river and around the country. I also arrested counterfeit document vendors and narcotics traffickers.

Narcotics trafficking and immigration issues are so enmeshed along the border that it is hard to separate the two. They also cause a huge risk to the safety of our citizens. According to a report released by the National Drug Intelligence Center (NDIC) in 2011, many cartel members continue immigrating legally to the United States or traveling with visas obtained at our foreign diplomatic missions, bringing their culture of bloodshed with them. The NDIC report states the cartels are operating in 1,286 cities throughout the United States, particularly in the Southwest. This is a genuine threat to our communities.

Violence between drug cartels has resulted in the deaths of more than thirty-seven thousand people in Mexico since 2006. Mexican president Felipe Calderón's government has spent hundreds of millions of pesos to crackdown on the syndicates. In retaliation, the drug lords have ordered the assassinations of hundreds of local and federal members of law enforcement, government agencies, and the courts.

More than twelve thousand soldiers and police are assigned to the Mexican border city of Juarez, where early in my career I disguised myself as a *pollo,* and where late in my career I uncovered an illegal visa-issuing scheme being perpetrated by employees of the U.S. consulate. Now Ciudad Juarez is nicknamed "the most dangerous city in the world." Despite the police presence, some 3,156 people, including many innocent civilians, were murdered there in 2010. In contrast, 2,080 civilians were killed in all of war-ravaged Afghanistan during the same time period. The manpower of the cartel armies is close to the manpower of the conscripted Mexican armed forces.

As was the case during my years as a young federal agent in Chicago, the dedication and determination of our law enforcement to break up the Mexican drug cartels' death grip on Chicago and other U.S. cities is unyielding. Some of those indicted are fugitives, but sooner or later they, too, will get their justice.

Drug dealers and human smugglers are parasites in our country, but they are not representative of the millions of immigrants, legal and illegal, who have settled here. I feel confident that 97–98 percent of those who come to our country become hardworking residents and citizens, striving to provide a decent living for their families, education for their children, and a safe place to live. They teach their children the ideals of what this country stands for, and as history has shown, many have been willing to die to defend this great nation.

There is no better example than a twenty-two-year-old lance corporal in the Marines, Jose Gutierrez, who in 2003 was among the first U.S. casualties of the Iraq War. He had grown up in an orphanage in his native Guatemala after his parents died. When he was fourteen, he made the two-thousand-mile trek to the U.S. border by riding fourteen different freight trains across Mexico. He was detained at the border by U.S. agents but allowed to stay. Our country does not deport minors who arrive without family, and he became a ward of the court in Los Angeles and placed in a foster home. He learned English, graduated from high school, and at eighteen got his residency documents before joining the U.S. Marines. He died in a firefight in Iraq on March 21, 2003, giving his life for the country that had given him everything.

Since 2001, the United States has granted citizenship to sixty-five thousand immigrants serving in our armed forces. I posthumously awarded citizenship to AnaLaura Esparza, another casualty of the Iraq War. Only twenty-two years old at the time of her death, she had immigrated to the United States when she was thirteen and was the only child of two legal immigrants originally from Monterrey, Mexico.

There are many role models in the Hispanic population who have worked hard and become community leaders and major contributors. Jose Hernandez worked the migrant fields with his family, just as I did, when he was young and went on to become an astronaut and fly on the space shuttle.

I understand people's reasons for coming to our great country but even in my understanding, I will not accept lax enforcement of our immigration laws at our borders and in our country's interior. Both must remain strong, as they are vital to our national security. And allowing them to gain employment once they are here makes us just as culpable.

This migration will not stop until our government takes the appropriate steps and corrective action, while at the same time other governments take responsibility for their own people. I don't see this happening in the near future.

Immigration reform and enforcement are complicated issues. I am proud to have represented and worked for the U.S. Border Patrol and the U.S. Immigration and Naturalization Service, alongside many fine officers and support personnel. As a field officer and in subsequent leadership positions, I led our agency in accomplishments never before achieved and unmatched since.

The illegal immigrant population in the United States has increased dramatically despite measures undertaken before and after the creation of the Department of Homeland Security in 2003. With up to fifteen million illegal immigrants in the country, it is a polarizing issue, with some states introducing legislation that grants immigration powers to state and local law enforcement authorities to determine immigrant age of individuals they encounter. Other groups demand legislation reform that would grant a path to citizenship for millions already in the country illegally.

Building the wall along portions of the southwestern border, and introducing laws at the state level, which some perceived as anti-immigration, have done little to address the issue of what to do with those who are already here. The laws that have been introduced come without funding to carry them out. The reality is that no efforts will ever be made by the federal government to arrest and deport these millions.

One side claims that no immigration reform will pass until the borders are "secure," but they have no real answer for what that means. In fact, millions of illegal immigrants enter with valid visas granted at U.S. diplomatic missions abroad. Despite the best efforts of consular officers who interview applicants for visas, recipients overstay their visas' expiration.

While there are those who seek to enter our country to do us harm, the great majority of immigrants come to this country looking to make a better life for themselves and their loved ones. As long as they are able to obtain employment, those who are in the country illegally will remain here and many more will come.

In his most recent state of the state speech, Texas governor Rick Perry stated "we must establish criminal penalties for employers who knowingly hire workers who are here in violation of immigration law." Yet the only legislative push Governor Perry made was for an "anti–sanctuary city" bill that he declared an "emergency," without being able to name a single sanctuary city. What happened to the criminal penalties he mentioned during his speech? Could it be that some of the more generous contributors to Governor Perry and members of his party are none other than businesses who depend on immigrant labor, such as in the construction, agriculture, and restaurant industries?

The Obama Administration, on the other hand, increased employer audit to ensure that they were complying with immigration requirements or they would face civil penalties. The administration was on track to deport larger numbers of immigrants than the previous administration. While this might sound formidable, it hardly addressed the issue or put a dent in the illegal immigrant population in the United States. Are these merely symbolic actions to show that the administration is enforcing immigration laws, while also hoping to pass some type of friendly immigration reform, as was promised during the last campaign to appease the growing Hispanic electorate?

Recent attention has been given to wealthy Chinese women who fly to the United States to give birth in this country, so the child will be a United States citizen. The "anchor baby" concept, too, has become a rather contentious issue. Our constitution guarantees citizenship for anyone born in this country except in certain diplomatic status cases. Should this practice be allowed?

I am not supportive of someone wanting to travel to our country for this specific purpose, but we are a country of laws and our constitution guarantees this right. Unless the Constitution is amended, "anchor babies" will be U.S. citizens.

For the record, children cannot petition for their parents to become legal residents until they turn twenty-one, so giving birth to a child here does not provide any type of special status for parents.

For some time now, several members of Congress and the present administration have supported passage of the Dream Act. This legislation would allow children who were brought illegally into the country at a young age, and have been raised and educated here, to pursue legal status after completing their education, and even be permitted to join the military. Over a period of time, their status would regularize to permanent resident and eventually, after many years, they could become citizens.

Immigrants' advocates say that these children came here through no fault of their own, have assimilated into our society, have received an education, and have a lot to offer our country—all reasonable arguments. I am not in complete agreement that we should reward those who broke the law to come into our country, even if they were minors. But I also know that we need to use common sense and be reasonable.

There are estimated to be two million people who would be affected by the Dream Act. We must come up with a resolution and in the end, I know we will. Let's no longer use the notion of waiting "until our borders are secure" as an excuse.

Easy solutions to our immigration issues are worthy of sensible debate. These are times that require utmost vigilance at our borders and in our consulates where visas are issued. The dedication of the men and women whom we entrust with our national security cannot be overstated. But there are no easy answers.

Acknowledgments

IF I COULD, I would thank and list every friend, family member, and former colleague who believed in me and was instrumental to my success and making this book possible. For those whom I fail to thank by name, my apologies, but know that you are in my heart.

I must first express my love and admiration for my mother, Esperanza Acosta. If every single person in America had her work ethic and "never give up" attitude, we would be an even greater nation. She was not perfect, but from her I learned that I could accomplish anything I set out to do. I thank my father, Salvador, for his belief in me and his encouragement despite our meager resources and opportunities as well as Jesus "Chuy" Prieto, an honorable, hardworking man I am proud to call my father-in-law.

My childhood teachers, Lucia Rede Madrid and Edmundo Madrid, instilled in me the value of reading. Through their encouragement, I learned about the greatness of our country and gained my desire to travel the world. I am proud to say that I followed their advice and have done just that.

Thanks to Marcelo Marini, a great television personality and dedicated servant of our community as well as a Spanish television pioneer in Houston, who listened to my stories and encouraged me to start writing them. I send my appreciation to Irma Diaz-Gonzalez for her support and community leadership as well as Jacob Monty, Eddie Seng, Abelardo Matamoros, Abel Sanchez, Ghulam Bombaywala, and Terry Shaikh. My gratitude to Renzo Heredia from Univision Radio and Grace Olivares for their great support and their belief in community service. Dr. Adan Rios will always be in our hearts for his help during a very trying time. To Carol Pereyra McKinney and Jose Pereyra for patiently reading my chapters and welcoming us into their homes. I cannot thank Carol enough for working for hours on end, helping me with my first book proposal and introducing me to a great literary agent. My sincere appreciation to Alice Peck and David Marion Wilkinson, great writers and believers, who were so instrumental in getting my project going.

I am honored to have been part of the U.S. Immigration and Naturalization Service, a proud organization never given adequate support, resources, or latitude, because of a lack of political will to let us fully do our jobs. Yet I can say without hesitation that our agency was second to none in protecting our great nation because of the many dedicated professional men and women who proudly served. It is my hope that these cases and success stories will provide a glimpse of the dedication and great accomplishments of our agency, even without the appropriate resources. We believed in our mission.

Ted Giorgetti was a great leader in Chicago who had a lasting influence on me. Thank you, Brian Perryman, for insisting that I become an all-around professional officer, not just an undercover agent. I have no doubt your wise counsel played a great role in helping me reach the pinnacle position of a field officer. I can never thank Roland Chasse enough for believing in me and taking me under his wing to take down the biggest and best counterfeiter our agency had ever arrested while I was a trainee, and for then working with me to tackle some of the biggest counterfeiting operations in Chicago.

It was so great to have Chicago police officer Greg Courchene and his wife, Shirley, as our neighbors in our first house in Chicago. I owe them so much for looking out for my young family during my travels and undercover operations. They were a guiding light for us, and we deeply admire them and their wonderful family.

To Arthur L. Nieto, a great friend and a great supporter, always willing to roll out regardless of the time or where we needed to go. My gratitude to Travis Everitt for unselfishly providing self-defense training for U.S. Marines at the U.S. Embassy in Mexico City at no cost because he wanted to do his part. I thank Mariela Melero for her leadership and commitment to make our agency the best and for helping me to become a contributing member of our community.

I attribute much of my success to the many fine agents who believed in me and worked tirelessly with me on these missions. A special word of gratitude to Special Agent Gil-

Acknowledgments

bert Wise, my partner in two huge human smuggling cases. May he rest in peace. A nod to Dionisio "Dennis" Lopez, the original electronic guru of our agency, who accomplished so much with so little, and to Jerry Goodman, an exceptional leader not afraid to tackle the big ones. David Garcia, Manny Perez, and David Ramirez were great officers. I thank them as well as Alfonso Pineda, my assistant officer in charge in Monterrey, Mexico, and Ben Aguirre, who headed our office in Ciudad Juarez. Jorge Eisermann, officer in charge in Guatemala, was an exceptional and dedicated agent, as was Salvador Briseno and Manny Flores, heads of our offices in Quito and Panama, respectively. Eddie Sotomayor and Abraham Lugo were hardworking representatives of our agency in El Salvador. I am indebted to three great Foreign Service national investigators, Jorge Garibay, Mauro Huerta, and Ricardo Reyes. A special thanks to Amalia Delgado, a proud American whose story must someday be told and injustice righted.

I was fortunate to work under Dan Solis while he headed the Bangkok District, as well as learning and having the great support of Greg B. Smith. Susan Vasquez was a great and gutsy undercover partner, and I thank her for those qualities and her dedication. Patrick Comey was an excellent partner I could depend on, and I am proud to call him my friend, as well as Warren Lewis, our district director in Washington, D.C., who was instrumental in helping me set up procedures to prosecute criminals operating outside our boundaries, a program still in use today. Carlos Salazar, Marc Sanders, Luis Massad, and Carlos Archuleta were hardworking officers whose support I valued. And how could I not thank Manuel

"Manny" Avila, who spent a night with me in a Mexican jail, and Bert Avila, who worked so diligently to get me out safe and sound.

Marianne Kilgannon-Martz always believed in my projects, supporting them and fighting for them while serving on the Headquarters Staff in Washington, D.C. Those in federal law enforcement know it's no easy task.

A. J. Irwin was without a doubt one of the best agents of any federal law enforcement branch, and one of my closest friends. I was proud to serve with him in one of the most dangerous cases we worked inside the United States as well as throughout Latin America and the Caribbean. My compadre and close friend David Castañeda, a dedicated, fearless agent whom I had the honor of working with on some of the best and most successful cases, was the man for whom we named our youngest son.

Finally, an agent from my early days who worked so many cases with me throughout the years and whose friendship I cherished throughout my career. To this day he is like a brother to me—Gary Renick. Thank you, partner.

To my brothers and sisters, I treasure the closeness, the sacrifices, the joys, and all we have gone through together. I am proud of each and every one of you—Magdalena Hendrix, Minnie Hartnett, Delma Acosta, Alicia Anaya, Teresa Rodriguez, Rebecca Betz, Mary De La Rosa, Fernando Acosta, Abelardo Acosta, Leonardo Acosta, Salvador Acosta, Arturo Acosta, and Arnulfo Acosta, may he rest in peace.

I appreciate the support of my brothers-in-law Andy Parsley, and his wife, Liz, and Jesse Parsely, as well as my sisters-in-law, Maria del Rosario Parsley, Betty Cunningham, and her husband, Virgle, and finally, Billie Davis and her late husband, Jerry.

I am fortunate to have Lisa Pulitzer, one of the best in the industry, join me as my coauthor. I thank her and her editor, Martha Smith, for their patience and for listening to all my stories as we wrote this book.

This book would not be possible were it not for the great literary agent I am so fortunate to have—B. G. Dilworth. Thank you, B.G., for your faith and support, and for never, ever giving up. You obviously share my motto: *Never take no for an answer.*

To the most wonderful children a parent can have—Gabe Acosta and his wife, Veronica Rodriguez; Keith Acosta and his wife; Cindy Cerrillo; Michelle Acosta and her husband; Michael Moore; and my youngest son, David Acosta, a proud agent and like his brother, Keith, a military officer. I am so proud of each of you. Thank you, sons, for seeing the greatness in our profession as each one of you followed in my footsteps. May you be safe as you protect and enforce the laws of this great country of ours.

My life would not be complete without the blessings of the most wonderful grandchildren a man could have—Gabriel Hipolito Acosta II, Talisa Acosta, Kayla Acosta, and Mia Moore Acosta. You bring so much love into our family.

This great journey would not have been possible without my best friend, soul mate, and believing partner whose love I cherish—my wife, Terrie. You believed in me from our very first date and your support meant more than you will ever realize as we journeyed around the world. Thank you for urging me over the years to write this book, being my first editor and reading the chapters over and over again, helping me with dates and events to make sure they were correct. I admire your courage in testifying in two federal trials on undercover cases that I worked on. You have been a true partner, and the best I can say is "I love you." This is our book.